T0127135

PRAISE FOR *RELATIONAL FINANCE*

Relational Finance saved my business. I initially engaged Ben's company to assist in an acquisition strategy. Admittedly, I did not have a full appreciation for Relational Finance at the time. Then, my industry entered the deepest downturn in decades. A typical transaction advisor would have been long gone, but Ben and his team rolled up their sleeves on cash management and forecasting capabilities. The shift in focus was fluid, natural, and fast enough to enable my company to go on offense despite the market challenges. Without Relational Finance, we would not have emerged on the other side as strong as we did.

LONNIE SMITH

President and Founder, Turnco

Ben Lehrer's work couldn't be more timely. Change is the only constant in business today, with data analytics and predictive capabilities top-of-mind across our CFO and CHRO Alliance membership base. Models such as Relational Finance serve a valuable role in incorporating finance capabilities into both day-to-day business management and long-term strategic planning. We know from our conversations and data that top-performing leaders are embracing the importance of a strong finance function in risk management, value creation, and successful deal-making.

NICK ARACO

CEO, AchieveNext

CEO and Founder, The CFO Alliance

I have evaluated well over one thousand companies during more than two decades of investing in privately-held businesses. The vast majority of these businesses have not conducted much if any financial planning and analysis (FP&A). This lack of FP&A capabilities results in a missed opportunity for business owners to understand their companies better by proactively harnessing their data, enabling them to build credible forecasts. Business owners could then convey their business and its prospects to private equity investors in a compelling, confident manner. Relational Finance is an innovative way for teams to access FP&A capabilities and look at their businesses through a different lens, improving business management today while enabling owners to map out the game plan to successfully engage with private equity or other buyers down the road. Ben's mission to open up these capabilities, particularly for smaller businesses in advance of a transaction, is a welcome addition to the marketplace.

JEFF TUDER

Partner, Ambina Partners

"Relational." Not a word I used to associate with finance. I have built and sold multiple companies, and have navigated the gauntlet of managing rapid growth, funding it, and ultimately going through deal processes. More and more I've come to realize the value of the finance function in each of my ventures. Ben's approach and the Relational Finance model is invaluable for guys like me, and I wish I had met him earlier. This book is mandatory reading for my team!

ANTHONY MILTON

CEO, TiltedConcepts

RELATIONAL FINANCE

THE **NEW MODEL** TO **ACCELERATE** GROWTH, **ATTRACT** CAPITAL, AND **MAXIMIZE** THE **VALUE** OF YOUR BUSINESS

RELATIONAL FINANCE

BETTER Teams **BETTER** Growth **BETTER** Deals

BENJAMIN J. LEHRER

Published by Advantage, Charleston, South Carolina.
Member of Advantage Media Group.

Printed in the United States of America.

10 9 8 7 6 5 4 3 2 1

ISBN: 978-1-64225-021-3
LCCN: 2018962595

Cover design by Melanie Cloth.
Layout design by Megan Elger.

For Archie and EV—my small and midsize children and the ever-growing return on my greatest investment.

TABLE OF CONTENTS

A WORD FROM THE AUTHOR

The entrepreneurial spirit can take hold at an early age. For many, the lemonade stand recalls the first thrill of bootstrapping an operation, from gathering materials around the kitchen, pleading with the Bank of Mom for a loan, and bartering with friends to spread the word. Perhaps we all share in a collective Rockwellian consciousness of showboating our lemons, water, and sugar as better than the kid's down the block. I would characterize the lemonade stand as possessing three simple yet core components of entrepreneurship: the intersection of opportunity, effort, and a good pitch.

I was one of those kids. Perhaps you were as well. I got hooked on the ol' sweet and sour and still have not had enough. After the "sidewalk" school of business, I moved on to the Wharton School of Business, and then Wall Street. Before long I had become part and parcel of the giant institutional machines of investment banking, private equity, lending, and consulting. One lens conveys the world to me: finance. So much so, that on dates with my wife—when work and kids are off limits for conversation—we gleefully concoct business ideas for sport.

The mind is a fickle thing that sometimes takes us on a ride out of our own control. For instance, whenever I encounter a business of any kind, consciously or subconsciously I attempt to tear apart the model. Visiting the local salad assembly joint with me is either a joyous or terrifying experience, depending on how you're wired. The conversation might go, "How can they possibly run out of romaine? Did you see those people double up on protein and not tell the cashier? You know if they added an extra dressing guy, the line would move twice as fast. Imagine all the business they're losing by not having a to-go counter."

Perhaps this psychosis started on Wall Street. Working in different firms on various deals, through a bull market and a nasty recession, I found myself questioning the pillars of establishment around me. Clear to anyone analyzing the models, Wall Street is designed for large companies. The lemonade stands, the small and midsize businesses (SMBs), are being left behind, for they lack access to the finance expertise and capital that their larger brethren enjoy. I call this the SMB finance gap.

The lemonade CEO inside me was aggrieved. Here was this vast problem, a massive market opportunity, yet I didn't have the answer. A global financial crisis provided the requisite kick in the pants, and I founded my own firm, First Water, to figure this out. In listening to the aspirations and pain points of SMB leaders and owners, the answers took form. Not just the SMB finance gap, but the value of finance itself. Finance has a tedious reputation of being all about numbers. However, the best parts of finance show up in team culture, goal setting, and storytelling.

The value of storytelling cannot be underestimated and extends far beyond finance. When I was fourteen, I was fortunate to have the opportunity to become an Eagle Scout. To this day, it remains one of my fondest experiences and most meaningful accomplishments. As part of earning the Eagle rank, a scout has to develop, propose, and execute an Eagle project to benefit the local community. In my troop, many scouts planted flower beds, often at exclusive private schools in the area. That didn't strike a chord with me, so I did what any smart kid would do. I asked Mom.

My mother has a doctorate in healthcare social working, and at the time was connected to an AIDS hospice near our house. She suggested I go talk to them. I had never been to a hospice before, and I was shaken. It was around the holidays and, amid the difficult environment, there were no holiday decorations displayed. When I asked why, the staff told me they were too busy to devote the time.

This gave me an idea—I would create holiday decoration kits for the hospice that were packaged for each holiday to make it easy for the staff to store, decorate, and reuse. Additionally, since hospice residents were often too ill to provide physical gifts to their families around the holidays, we would gather donations of tape recorders and supplies so they could memorialize their stories for their loved ones. The staff loved the idea and welcomed my efforts.

Next, I had to pitch the project to the scoutmaster board and get approval. I went proudly in front of the board and stated, "For my Eagle Scout project, I want to do something more meaningful than plant flowers." I told them about my project plans and about the support I had received from the hospice workers. Gong! The proposal was rejected.

I made a fatal mistake. I neglected to realize that the sons of three (out of the five) scoutmasters on the board had already completed Eagle Scout projects. As you may have guessed, they all planted flowers. I had told the wrong story to get the scoutmasters on board with my vision. Thankfully, after another iteration and pitch, they green-lighted my project. The hospice was thrilled, but that initial rejection has remained with me to this day.

> ***The wrong story can kill even the greatest idea, whereas a great story can breathe life into the simplest of concepts.***

Today I help entrepreneurs manage, grow, fund, and sell their businesses with stories told through the lens of finance. The finance function of a business has five components: (1) data, (2) reporting, (3) projections, (4) planning, and (5) capital. Historically, SMBs were either priced out of these capabilities, limited to accessing them piecemeal, or were faced with having them tied to an immediate transaction requirement. That is no longer the case. Now I am proposing a new model, which I call Relational Finance.

Within this book we will explore the value of each of the five components of the finance function, introduce the Relational Finance model enabling SMBs to gain innovative access to finance capabilities, and discuss tactical ways to put those capabilities into practice.

I have worked with a variety of different businesses, but they all possess one important commonality that drives their success: their entrepreneurial spirit. This spirit is the heart of all great companies. This book is about marrying the entrepreneurial spirit with the access to finance capabilities that SMBs deserve. Finance provides the tools, processes, people, and capital that amplify and protect the entrepreneurial spirit.

The finance function is often ignored or underappreciated until it is too late. Early on, SMBs can survive and even prosper without the finance function for two reasons: (1) either leadership has great intuition, and/or (2) consistent growth has made it easier to navigate bumps in the road. Eventually, lack of sufficient finance capabilities will hurt every company. It's just a matter of time.

Within this book I present a fresh view, a redefinition of finance that makes it approachable, valuable, and actionable. This includes a look at how traditional finance models work and how Relational Finance is the optimal solution for SMBs to align and accelerate their growth and capital roadmaps by unleashing their finance function.

There are more businesses than ever before who need to hear this message. The baby boomer generation is retiring and the amount of businesses that need to be transitioned or sold is more than any other time in history. Currently, many of those businesses are not sellable because the owners have not prepared. There is a general misunderstanding of how the finance function ties into transaction goals. The stakes are high. Owners must get it right.

No matter the objective—whether it be increased profitability, revenue growth, or a future sale—you will find useful material here that you can put into action in your business today.

As detailed in chapter 5, Relational Finance is defined as customized access to finance capabilities delivered through an engagement framework which promotes alignment of interests between company and advisor. By investing in finance and leveraging Relational Finance, businesses can drive better teams, better growth, and better deals while attracting the right capital and partners to achieve their goals. This book is the catalyst to advance the finance dialogue within the SMB community. Enjoy it, harness it, and unleash your finance function!

CHAPTER 1

A CLOSER LOOK AT FINANCE

There are many reasons why people decide to start a business. Business owners are creators, passion seekers, and legacy builders. While we all agree with this, many realize that most SMB owners do not begin as experts in business management or finance. In our great country of limitless possibilities, it doesn't matter, at least not initially. However, there comes a point in a company's growth cycle where business management processes, both from a people perspective and finance capabilities perspective, must be prioritized. This inflection point is often characterized by owners and leadership teams who realize they have bitten off more than they can chew. Chances are, if you're reading this book, you may have reached that point or you may see it coming. Even if the needs are not immediately visible, we will talk about building blocks of team performance, growth, and transaction execution from which every business can benefit.

Business management, growth, and the opportunity for monetization can only go so far without understanding and utilizing the power of finance. It is one of the most powerful tools a business owner can and must harness.

Every single decision a business owner makes has a financial component. Finance is the only function that is truly intertwined with every other function in a business. In spite of this, it is the least understood business function of SMB leaders and owners who often have very little finance exposure or expertise before starting a business.

For that very reason, I am going to break down the finance function into five key components that we will focus on in this book: (1) data, (2) reporting, (3) projections, (4) planning, and (5) capital. Each component depends mutually on the others. I describe these components as a *finance spectrum.* When utilized properly, finance is the vein that connects teams with data and companies with capital. We will explore what that means throughout this book.

Finance is the vein that connects teams with data and companies with capital.

Until now, there has never been a service model that delivers this full spectrum of finance capabilities without major strings attached, such as an upfront transaction (having to "do the deal" first). Consequently, SMBs have traditionally been forced to access the spectrum components piecemeal through different traditional finance models. Not only does this lack cost effectiveness for SMBs, but it also creates a communication barrier. Traditional consulting firms do not engage in capital transactions, and merger and acquisition firms do not specialize in synthesizing data. I knew there had to be a way to create a "one-stop shop" and bring the entirety of the finance spectrum under one umbrella.

THE TRADITIONAL MODELS OF FINANCE

Since early adolescence, finance has fascinated me—so much so that I've devoted my entire career to understanding it and helping others do the same. When I refer to traditional finance models in this book, I want you to think about working directly with advisors and capital providers. Advisors are project consultants, interim/fractional leaders, and transaction intermediaries like investment banks. Capital providers are lenders, investors, and buyers—those who provide capital to grow and monetize the value in your business.

Traditional finance models serve an important and valuable role in the marketplace, and my goal is not to fault them. Rather, I want to help you understand that the manner in which these models are structured can make it particularly difficult for SMBs to access.

With that said, let's take a closer look at how traditional finance models work:

---

1. **Traditional finance models have a rigid engagement framework.** They are created in such a way that business owners must know exactly what they want, now and in the future. In my experience, SMB owners rarely know *exactly* what they want or need when it comes to finance. Primarily, they are unaware of all the options available to them. To further complicate matters, goals and objectives change. It's called life. What I have come to understand as a business owner myself is that this is simply the reality of running a business. Traditional

finance models do not account for this pliability which becomes a problem when owners have questions or lack clarity.

2. **Traditional models are structured to serve their own business and economic models, not necessarily the goals or objectives of SMBs.** Traditional finance models are businesses themselves and, not surprisingly, they are focused on their own growth and economies of scale. This contributes to their rigidity as they define the rules of engagement. When there are limited ways to access certain expertise, the experts call the shots. What is best for their revenues, profits, and scale might not be fully aligned with the success of their clientele.
3. **Traditional finance models have an inherent conflict relating to transactions and fees.** Transactions are not fundamentally bad. Quite the opposite! The primary problem is that many traditional finance models require upfront or immediate transactions. Therefore, transactions become the requirement for SMBs to gain access to certain professional expertise. This is particularly true for transaction intermediaries and capital providers.
4. **Traditional finance models tend to pull the best talent upstream because of compensation associated with transaction or asset size.** The economics of these models are correlated with transaction size, fund size, or hourly fees. Talented financial professionals gravitate toward bigger deals, bigger funds, or higher hourly rates. Therefore, larger businesses have access to a more talented pool of professionals, and there is some truth to getting what you pay for. This creates a

problem for SMBs who do not have the same financial resources or business profile to attract and access the financial talent they equally deserve.

So, what are SMBs to do? This was the question I asked early on in my career. I observed firsthand how SMB owners were sometimes left out in the cold. Finance capabilities and capital access are equally critical to all businesses regardless of size. In fact, the argument can be made that SMBs have a greater need for these than large companies, as they often operate with less financial wiggle room.

This conundrum fueled my desire to spend the rest of my career championing SMB owners and teams. I believe there is a better way to bring the same finance capabilities down-market so that SMBs could more effectively pursue growth, raise capital, and complete transactions.

WHO AM I FIGHTING FOR?

Now that you understand *what* I'm fighting for, I will tell you *who* I'm fighting for—SMB owners and leaders. Owners often call my company, First Water, at a critical inflection point in their business. Future potential growth and/or transaction objectives look very different than today. They are heading into new territory. I shall elaborate by sharing the profiles, inflection points, and pain points of three different SMB owner personas. Reflecting the majority of those that I work with, I categorize them as follows: (1) the Opportunity Maker, (2) the Opportunity Taker, and (3) the Monetizer. Take a moment to determine with whom you most identify.

The Opportunity Maker

This profile describes every entrepreneur whose goal is starting a business and creating a proven, sustainable business model. It is fair to say that the Opportunity Maker is the persona baseline. Within every company, the entrepreneurial spirit is best defined by the Opportunity Maker's persona.

The tipping point for this persona is when success is achieved and there is a desire to pick up the pace. This is an aggressive business owner who seeks superhero status with eyes set on big market opportunities to be achieved quickly. This business owner often invests profits back into the business and is willing to run unprofitably for a period of time, occasionally raising outside debt or equity capital in order to take advantage of new opportunities.

- **Pain points:** Multiple pain points must be overcome to achieve superhero status. The Opportunity Maker often fails to foresee the path to achieve desired growth. This entrepreneur lacks the analytical expertise to credibly map out how much money is required or the embedded risks. Opportunity Makers require guidance to understand capital sizing and capital structuring—how much is needed and what kind. Often, they have never worked with an institutional capital partner. With wise reason for concern, Opportunity Makers realize that bringing outside money into the business is more than capital, it's a partnership. The incorrect choice could result in misalignment regarding the future of the business. A wrong decision results in years and years of pain, if not failure.
- **Inflection point:** Opportunity Makers can no longer internally fund aggressive growth goals. They must

position and execute on outside capital from a partner who is aligned with their vision and growth roadmap. To get it right, they need a forward-looking view to determine the right capital amount and structure, and to identify and attract the right partner(s).

The Opportunity Taker

This profile describes a business owner who is stable and profitable, has a nice flow of prospects, and is eager to continue growing and operating the business. This entrepreneur may not be focused on—but seeks to take advantage of—opportunities as they arise even if there is currently no direct visibility to what those opportunities may be.

- **Pain points:** Despite their successes to date, Opportunity Takers struggle with the day-to-day financial management of their business. Consequently, they carry around a great deal of stress. Lacking a long-term plan, the owner's family relies upon the business and worries about instability and "what if"s. Being too busy and unprepared to take advantage of new opportunities results in overwork. Better business visibility and planning processes will reduce the number of surprises, which often surface at the worst of times.
- **Inflection point:** To sleep more soundly at night, the Opportunity Taker must position the business and team for less risk, thereby becoming better prepared to seize organic or opportunistic growth opportunities. A growth roadmap is critical to ensure the business is going after the right opportunities for long-term objectives. Opportunity Takers realize that a support system (or partner) is necessary

to take the business to the next level. The goal is to take steps toward a more meaningful quality of life with the confidence that each step is toward the long-term summit.

The Monetizer

The Monetizer is an SMB owner considering a business exit, regardless of whether the timing of such exit is defined or not. The eventual objective is the monetization of the value created within the business. The Monetizer is concerned about valuation, an exit and transition strategy, and the impact on employees.

- **Pain points**: Lacking previous experience in selling a business and understanding how buyers will assess the company, the Monetizer's primary concerns are the unknowns. These include the emotional impact of walking away, the risk of leaving money on the table, or not knowing whether a transition period is required (and for how long). Monetizers may not know what specifically makes their businesses sellable, and they do not know what the people on the other side of the table are thinking. The pressure is on to optimize the value of the business, and then extract that value.
- **Inflection point:** Monetizers know that timing is everything. They have more options when the timeline for selling the business is within three years rather than three weeks. It is difficult to sell a business that is fully dependent on the owner; a large part of the value of the business is walking out the door. The path to success is through the creation of a flourishing, standalone operation. The goal is maximization, not just monetization.

While each of these profiles, pain points, and inflection points are different, they all have three very important things in common: (1) they possess a forward-looking mentality; (2) they realize they cannot accomplish their goals without the right knowledge, tools, and business processes; and (3) they are unsure of where to begin. Many owners assume each of the three personas over the course of the entrepreneurial journey.

SMB owners who manage their pain points and inflection points have the best chance of crushing their competition and achieving the outcomes they desire. The finance function is an integral tool for pulling it all together. There is just one big problem, and it is the motivator behind this book.

Business owners often become confused about which direction to go because traditional finance models are not set up for SMBs to access. Larger businesses have easier access to credit and more financial resources to invest in their infrastructure and teams. I am not suggesting that this makes larger businesses bad. It is simply the SMB reality, and it's why SMBs must invest in their finance functions. The sooner the better.

This book enables SMB owners and leaders to outpace their competition by leveraging my new approach to finance. Finance access is not yet widely attainable for SMBs, and there is a first mover opportunity to hit the gas pedal. On the contrary, the absence of a finance function is a major contributor to why SMBs fall behind.

Apart from deficiencies in a product or service, a lack of finance capabilities is arguably the number one reason why businesses fail. It is not the fault of SMB owners for not understanding finance. After all, the majority of entrepreneurs have never worked for the finance or accounting teams of a big corporation. It *is* the responsibility of owners to educate themselves along the way. That is the primary motivation for this book, and I'm happy to have you on this journey with me.

ALIGNED AND COST-EFFECTIVE FINANCE EXPERTISE

Before starting First Water, I spent years racking my brain, convinced that there had to be a better way for SMBs to access finance expertise. I had seen plenty of businesses have a smattering of successes and failures. My exposure to the world of finance through different business models, ranging from start-ups to Fortune 50 companies, together with the skillset I have cultivated, has made me a uniquely qualified professional. There are not many people who have worked in an investment bank, a private equity firm, a commercial bank, a consulting firm, and within small businesses. In essence, I bring five different finance perspectives into one seat. In the context of being in the market and constantly talking with business owners, I had all the experience necessary to put the pieces together. I realized there was a real opportunity for innovation by providing SMBs access to finance expertise aligned with all these different perspectives. But how?

I was not initially sure, but I was determined to figure it out. I knew there were two non-negotiable characteristics which must be embedded for my new model to work as I envisioned.

First, SMBs must have access to a model that has the flexibility to pivot. As I alluded to earlier, goals and objectives often change in a business. Therefore, any new model would need to add value in a variety of different ways. Ask any professional services or investment business today and they will tell you that having flexibility makes a business harder to scale. However, scalability was never the heart of my goal. Everything in our world today screams disruption and scalability, but I realized that if I was truly going to create a better solution for SMBs, then having the flexibility to structure relationships around unique solutions would be the only way to preserve the integrity of the model. As an aside, I believe the majority of businesses should be structured this way, not just finance models. Service businesses should always focus on finding the right answers first, and then structuring the relationship to align with those answers.

Second, SMBs must have access to a model that fosters deep, long-term relationships. This does not keep my firm from engaging in shorter-term projects or immediate transaction opportunities, but it is a lot easier to go from long-term to short-term than the other way around. I hold firm to the fact that I earn trust by always acting like a partner, sometimes even becoming a true partner, and replacing the benefits of scalability with the increased upside potential of directly participating in value creation and monetization.

Flexibility with a long-term relationship focus is a powerful win-win, both for my clients and my firm. I have always believed in the importance of focusing on good people with good businesses. In doing this, I can pursue opportunities through a model that truthfully puts people first. I believe that conversations that start with goals and stay focused on goals (even as they change) are the best way to build, sustain, and grow mutually beneficial relationships.

The time is ripe for this message. With the baby boomer generation thinking about retirement, we have arrived at a point where more SMBs must be sold than any other time in history. Relational Finance offers SMBs access to a differentiated capability set which they never had previously.

As the message of this new finance model begins to spread, I believe Relational Finance will eventually become the default expectation of SMBs. This is the future of finance. Ultimately, all businesses are going to have better access to finance capabilities and capital. I am so committed to this future that I am making the model available to any would-be competitors for the price of a book. And I welcome that, because that is what the market needs and deserves.

Until now, SMBs have not had a sounding board in the traditional finance landscape. Now they do. I have found that by focusing on the core components of conversations around goals, aligning relationships around goals, and building trust over time by adding value, everyone wins because we achieve goals crafted together and we are economically aligned around those goals.

The question SMB owners need to ask themselves is, "Do I want to be ahead of the curve or do I want to wait until its standard practice?"

A BETTER WAY

The traditional finance models are not broken, and there are plenty of appropriate times to use them. However, traditional models view businesses as a transactional opportunity: one project, one transaction, one deal. By their very design, their framework makes it almost impossible to put relationships first.

Furthermore, SMBs who are forced into traditional finance models need to understand that all the expertise sits on the other side of the table. This is a fundamental problem because of the inherent conflicts within these models. These conflicts put SMBs at a disadvantage, requiring them to devote a significant amount of time and resources to level the playing field prior to engaging. The reality is SMBs cannot rely on "the person sitting across the table" to give them an unbiased view of what they should do. SMBs need to be armed with as much knowledge as possible. They need "other side of the table" expertise on their side of the table.

SMBs represent the biggest subset of businesses in our country, and yet they are up against these inherent conflicts within the traditional finance models. This restricts them from vetting their options and efficiently executing on their growth and capital roadmaps. The need is great for someone who can simultaneously help them drill down into their performance data, take control of their outlook, collaboratively plot the roadmap, and help them execute on growth and transaction initiatives. Businesses that invest in finance stand the best chance of growing and protecting what they've built. To take that one step further, I usually advise owners that businesses rarely (if ever) fail because they were run very well. But, the market can blow up, an owner can pick a bad partner, or a company can bring the wrong type or amount of capital into the business.

The reality is SMBs cannot rely on "the person sitting across the table" to give them an unbiased view of what they should do. SMBs need to be armed with as much knowledge as possible. They need "other side of the table" expertise on their side of the table.

This book advances the finance dialogue within the SMB community to help improve day-to-day quality of life and reduce business risk. I want owners and leaders to see how they can better keep a finger on the pulse of their business and maximize the ability to reach goals faster, more efficiently, and safely by prioritizing the value of their finance function.

A QUEST FOR CHANGE

Now that we have identified these limitations of access, we can thoroughly dig into my quest for change—one that has the potential to transform the way in which SMBs leverage their finance function and other related capabilities.

I believe that business owners deserve:

- a solid understanding of the finance function and why it is valuable;
- the ability to harness all five components of the finance function (data, reporting, projections, planning, and capital) from a single source;
- knowledge of available options and confidence in decision-making; and
- cost-effective finance expertise aligned with *their* goals.

There is a fundamental reason why many business owners do not receive what they deserve, and it has nothing to do with traditional finance models. Instead, it has everything to do with the business owner. More often than not, an SMB owner does not prioritize finance. Only after buying into the value of finance can owners seek out the access they deserve. Investing in finance, and incorporating it into both decision-making and planning, gives business owners the best chance of achieving their goals.

In the next chapter, we are going to look at the evolution of the entrepreneurial spirit. We will explore the transition that must occur from entrepreneur to business leader. I will illustrate how the entrepreneurial spirit can go from being an owner's biggest asset to most dangerous liability if finance is not prioritized early enough in the journey.

CHAPTER 2

FROM ENTREPRENEUR TO BUSINESS LEADER

The entrepreneurial spirit is at the foundation of all great companies. An entrepreneur has a can-do, problem-solving attitude that rallies people around a mission. As a result, nothing stops a spirited entrepreneur from breaking down doors, marching on in, and making things happen. It does not matter how difficult that process may be. Unyielding optimism, determination, grit, and perseverance are powerful traits which empower entrepreneurs to create something from nothing.

These are the hallmarks of the formation of great companies. The entrepreneurial spirit says, "I'm going to jump off a cliff, then figure out how to construct a parachute before I hit the rocks below." By nature, entrepreneurs are really good at jumping off cliffs. In fact, the successful ones do it over and over again. The more they prove to themselves that they can figure it out on the way down, the more they want to do it again. If you're a business owner, you know exactly what I'm talking about!

Now the kicker. While this risk-taking mentality is essential for entrepreneurs to start and grow their businesses, this same spirit can be equally dangerous. As businesses grow and the opportunities they pursue get bigger, so do the risks involved. Therefore, all business owners reach key inflection points (like the ones I outlined in chapter 1) where grit and perseverance no longer carries them through. In order to keep growing their businesses, they take bigger and bigger risks. Whether they are going after a monster customer or building a new facility, big wagers are being placed. These inflection points are catalysts for why a business may seek outside help.

The best way to get bigger is to act bigger. Owners reach a point where the needs of the business outstrip existing skills. This is not a bad thing. It is an important tipping point. They realize that if their business grows past a certain stage or size, they will not be able to manage (or maybe micromanage) the same way. They can no longer jump without a parachute and believe everything will be okay. Eventually they are going to have a problem.

The best way to get bigger is to act bigger.

As businesses grow, they become more complicated to manage. The "widget master" entrepreneur who started off because he believed he could make something, sell something, or package something better now faces some tough realities. While market opportunities become greater, so do the risks required to seize those opportunities. The margin for error decreases across the board. The entrepreneur must make the transition to a business leader.

I would like to offer you an example of how this applies to a business. Let's take the owner of a manufacturing facility who has grown annual sales to $15 million. The view from the office overlooking the shop floor clearly shows what employees are doing. When something goes wrong on the floor, the owner can come down to fix it.

But now, there is a new opportunity. A large prospective customer has expressed interest in engaging the company, which would double the company's current revenue. In order to serve the customer, this owner would need to open up two fully-equipped shops in other cities to handle the customer's local needs. These other cities happen to be on the target expansion list. Confidence is strong that the capacity of the new shops will be filled shortly after bringing on this new big customer. By opening and filling the new shops, with this new customer and others, the company could evolve into a $50 million revenue business. Sounds like an easy decision.

The owner pushes the proverbial start button and does the following:

- commits to delivering the volume to the customer (who is now 50 percent of the company's total business);
- signs leases for the new facilities;
- secures a bank loan to acquire/install the equipment for the new facilities;
- brings on an equity partner to provide the capital needed to staff and ramp up the new facilities;
- hires three facility managers, including one for the first shop;
- sets off to secure more new customers to fill up the new facilities; and
- hires the operating staff for the new facilities.

This manufacturer has positioned the business to get substantially bigger very quickly. Great, right?

Let's pump the brakes. While this opportunity is transformational for the business, it represents a change to the operations and management of the business. One customer has single-handedly changed the entire outlook of the company. That may not seem like a bad thing, but if that customer places a customized order with the manufacturer and then goes bankrupt, the manufacturer stands to be left with a bunch of inventory that is not sellable. Clearly, this might not be a situation where the manufacturer can persevere and figure it out on the fly. The sudden descent off a major cliff occurs. The question is this: are the necessary parts and tools available to construct the parachute?

I often talk with owners and leaders who have not anticipated the ripple effects of windfall opportunities, and it is not all roses. This new customer that the manufacturer has taken on now disproportionately impacts all operations, including inventory stocking, production scheduling, price negotiations, and cash requirements because of lead times and payment terms.

This manufacturer can no longer spend time monitoring the shop floor. Now, filling up the new facilities becomes the priority. While it was the owner who previously fixed production problems, that critical task is now in the hands of others—three new facility managers.

There are more contractual commitments with long-term leases and debt financing. The lease, interest, and principal payments must be made timely each month. Overhead has substantially increased with the addition of staff. In addition, the new equity partner is in the fold and that partner wants a say in key business decisions to ensure a return on the investment.

The world has changed dramatically for this manufacturer. Margins for error have declined significantly despite the benefits of scaling up the business. There are additional financial commitments, altered leadership roles, and changes to the capital structure. If you are unfamiliar with that term, the *capital structure* is the mix of debt and equity within a business. The capital structure details the prioritization (also known as seniority) of cash flow, profits, and sale proceeds. For example, debt typically gets its money back before the equity holders get paid.

This is only a hypothetical example that I wanted to share to illustrate the realities, opportunities, and challenges I see inside businesses every day.

In order for our manufacturer to be positioned for success, there are many questions to consider before pushing the start button. Here are a few:

- Will there be cash (funding) to cover all the payroll, overhead, inventory requirements for the additional customer(s)?
- How will the performance of the shop managers be supervised and how will they be held accountable?
- What happens if the new large customer terminates the relationship, or worse, goes bankrupt?
- While ramping up growth, will the company be profitable enough to cover debt payments to the bank and be clear of any loan covenants?
- Is the new equity partner aligned with the goals for the company?

- Will the manufacturer get a good deal for that new equity, or give up more than necessary?
- Can the manufacturer live with any new restrictions on salary or use of company funds that did not exist before having a lender or partner involved?

In my experience, these are the types of finance-related questions that SMB owners often neglect to fully explore. Most successful business owners have a different mind-set when they reach inflection points like this one. They realize that they must build a parachute before jumping off the cliff. If they cannot complete the parachute assembly, they at least know what the missing pieces are beforehand!

The finance function is one of those key pieces. The finance capabilities themselves represent the way businesses build their parachutes *before* hurling themselves off the cliff. There are lots of ways this manufacturer can mitigate risk, but that requires foresight. Therefore, a fair amount of upfront work must be done to characterize the risks. These efforts also inform how the owner negotiates with the new customer. For example, requests could be made for the customer to prepay orders, cap order size, or make progress payments along the way for larger orders. Note that it is hard to negotiate terms after the customer relationship has started!

The opportunity to double or triple in size may seem like a no-brainer on the surface, but it is never that clear cut. In the aforementioned example we saw how properly assessing the new customer opportunity required a deeper level of understanding. Much of that understanding flows through finance.

THE FOUR PROTECTIVE PILLARS

As SMB owners continue to build their businesses, they quickly find out that they are faced with bigger opportunities and bigger risks. Therefore, if they continue to approach opportunities with the same "bull in a china shop" attitude, eventually they will run into some problems. Once they reach this point, owners must question whether their problems are small enough to be tolerated. If they do not make any changes, the answer will become a resounding, "No!" A business owner can do everything right for years and then make one bad decision. One uncalculated risky jump could result in the business (and the owner) going splat!

> ***There are four protective pillars that must surround the entrepreneurial spirit to keep it from destroying itself: (1) tools, (2) processes, (3) people, and (4) capital. Each pillar helps to ensure that a business owner and team are marching toward the same goal and staying on track along the way. Together, they protect the entrepreneurial culture while transforming companies into business machines. These pillars should be in place in every business, big or small.***

While there is no such thing as growing a business risk-free (that's a bit of a paradox), risk reduction is achievable. The protective pillars are the difference between jumping off a cliff unprepared and jumping with a fully constructed parachute (or at least an instruction manual).

Consider our manufacturer again. With these protective pillars, the framework could be put in place to make the best decisions for the business, the team, and the owner. The alternative, executing blindly on a seemingly positive opportunity, is a dangerous path.

These pillars would have also helped ensure that our manufacturer and the team were marching toward the same goal by providing forward-looking capabilities. Proper foresight would have helped in building confidence that all the right questions were being asked, to see not only the giant opportunity, but also the potential threats as well.

Possessing the ability to monitor how things are going and making sure that a business operates within an acceptable risk tolerance is another benefit of the pillars. Business owners who recognize they are pushing outside their limits can adjust accordingly. Adjustments are a core component for all businesses to arrive at their desired destination as "safely" as possible. Knowing the risks is a critical step.

When I sit down with owners, I advise them that the best way to grow into the desired future is to run the business today as they would in the future. Owners should never wait until they reach their destination before putting those missing pieces into place. If they delay, those same pieces could prohibit them from achieving their goals.

Of course, even with these four protective pillars in place, business is still a risky proposition. Whatever drives entrepreneurs to get into business will not be the same factor that allows them to stay in business. This requires an evolution of the entrepreneurial spirit.

THE EVOLUTION OF THE ENTREPRENEURIAL SPIRIT

By this point, you are seeing how neglecting to rein in the aggressive risk-taking of the entrepreneurial spirit will eventually cause failure. It's simply a matter of time, right? Therefore, entrepreneurs must make a life-saving transition to business leaders, sooner rather than later!

Running a business well is marked by a few key shifts in the mind-set of an entrepreneur. There are moments of enlightenment that must take place in order for the entrepreneur to evolve and begin thinking like a business leader. Let's look at the most important ones:

- **Business leaders train their eyes to envision the future.** They understand that the skills that made them successful are not necessarily the same skills that will take them where they want to go. They realize that the management requirements and challenges of running a business that is a multiple of its current size are very different from the requirements and challenges that exist now. With this type of vision, they understand that the best way to reach their goals is to put the pieces in place to manage a larger business today.
- **Business leaders realize that time spent reacting is the worst use of time.** They are not content with "fire drill" cultures. In fact, they want to eliminate this type of activity as much as possible. To accomplish this, they prioritize the importance of processes, controls, and other proactive activities. As a result, business leaders are able to spend more time positioning the company for the future and less time reacting to what is going on in the present. It bears mentioning that while no business can ever completely

eliminate reactionary time, the more a business leader can minimize it, the better.

- **Business leaders finance today's business with the long-term in mind.** Leaders make capital decisions that are aligned with their long-term goals, while understanding how different capital partners analyze their businesses. They realize that an investment or a loan may come with strings attached, and they ensure those strings are not in conflict with their growth plans or long-term vision. The worst situation is taking whatever capital you can get, because you need it now. Although capital might fill a hole or take advantage of a short-term opportunity, the wrong kind of capital can set a business back for years.
- **Business leaders are continuously improving as managers.** High-performing businesses strive for continuous improvement, and business leaders understand how the finance function impacts the process. Leaders accept that they cannot continuously improve without the use of data, reporting, projections, and planning. These are key pieces that drive the cycle of tracking, analyzing, iterating, and improving. By prioritizing continuous improvement, business leaders create more engaged teams that can increase productivity and efficiency. Business leaders recognize that they cannot make lasting improvements or speed up the pace of those improvements without the right information flow and the ability to look forward. Therefore, business leaders ensure all progress and improvements are tracked and reported. They realize that without the flow of the right information, they cannot

understand how to project and plan in a way aligned with their goals.

- **Business leaders realize that growth requires more responsibility in the hands of others.** Business leaders ensure that their teams are engaged, aligned, accountable, and incentivized toward activities and results that drive the business forward. They understand how important it is for a team to be not only in the same boat, but also rowing in the same direction. I am not a fan of over-used clichés, but one I pound the table on is, "You can't manage what you can't measure." Business leaders define and track progress to avoid finger pointing of blame across their teams. They understand that mismanaged data creates a land grab for who deserves credit amongst a team, and that almost always results in a misaligned, fractured workforce.

I stated at the beginning of this chapter that the entrepreneurial spirit is at the foundation of all great companies, but foundations are designed to be built upon. As we wrap up this chapter, I hope you understand how the entrepreneurial spirit needs to evolve, all while preserving what makes it so valuable. In the next chapter, we will further explore why finance is often the Achilles heel of SMBs and how I am on a mission to change that.

CHAPTER 3

FINANCE: FRIEND OR FOE?

SMB owners live in a chaotic world. They are constantly learning on the fly and cobbling things together. In order to win, they must be strong at many things. They must have good products, great sales capabilities, finely tuned operations, and scalable business models with staying power. For the ones who figure out how to pull it all together, it is always impressive to watch.

However, winning in business sometimes means running lean on support. I recently sold a company that was in business for over thirty-five years and the owner was still cleaning the bathrooms. He had become very successful. So why was he still doing janitorial work? Simply put, he did not see the value in paying someone else do it.

This simple example points to a bigger, non-janitorial problem. SMBs are often inadequately staffed by the right kind of talent inside their businesses. Finance is no exception. In fact, I would argue that finance is the most neglected area and has the biggest shortage of talent among SMBs. In my experience, finance only tends to come up among SMBs when bad things happen. This type of reactionary response and mind-set puts business owners at a big disadvantage; finance becomes their Achilles heel. One wrong finance decision could derail an entire business.

While this may intimidate some, SMB owners are not like everyone else. They are accustomed to flying by the seat of their pants. However, this approach does not translate well to the finance function, especially as a business grows. If you have ever owned or operated a business before, I am sure you can relate. As a business experiences growth, almost everything becomes exponentially more complicated to manage.

I want business owners to understand that their ability to successfully manage their business as it is right now may be adequate. Assuming the business continues to grow, how a business currently exists will not be an indicator of where it might be a year or two from now. Therefore, deciding to prioritize finance is not a question of if, but when. SMBs have an opportunity to turn finance into one of their strengths—again, the earlier the better. Growing a business beyond its current state and positioning it as an attractive option for capital partners depends on it.

Deciding to prioritize finance is not a question of if, but when.

THE CLASSICAL DEFINITION OF FINANCE

The world of finance is often misunderstood. In general, when people think about finance, they think about Wall Street or accounting functions. They do not necessarily think about finance as its own corporate function. The critical (and often overlooked) role that finance plays in a business is exactly what we are going to explore in this chapter.

You may be surprised to discover that many companies, including significantly sized ones, do not always have dedicated finance teams. They may think they do through their accounting functions, but finance and accounting are not one and the same.

In order to understand the difference between the two, let's quickly look at *Merriam-Webster*'s definition of each: *Accounting* is "a system of recording and summarizing business and financial transactions and analyzing, verifying, and reporting the results," whereas *finance* is "a system that includes the circulation of money, the granting of credit, the making of investments, and the provision of banking facilities."[1]

While each of these functions is differentiated, neither one of these definitions explains the finance function as I believe it should exist inside a business. This is a contributor to a bigger problem. A clear definition of what finance should look like *inside* a business, as part of day to day management, is not readily available.

Finance breaks down into two core segments: **operational finance** and **corporate finance**. Operational finance, more commonly called financial planning and analysis (FP&A), is the data hub of the business. It is defined by functions such as data, reporting, projections, and planning. Operational finance tends to focus on profit and loss drivers, or the income statement. Corporate finance is the return on investment (ROI) hub of the business. It is defined by capital planning, investments, and transaction execution. It is the balance

1 *Merriam-Webster*, s.v. "accounting (n.)," accessed August 2018, https://www.merriam-webster.com/dictionary/accounting; *Merriam-Webster*, s.v. "finance (n.)," accessed August 2018, https://www.merriam-webster.com/dictionary/finance.

sheet and capital structure driver. To put it in context, Wall Street is the supreme corporate finance machine—it's all about deals.

THE FINANCE SPECTRUM

I describe the five key components that connect operational and corporate finance as existing on a *finance spectrum*, with the components themselves making up the finance function of an organization. The finance function is comprised of: *data*, *reporting*, *projections*, *planning*, and *capital*. Each of these five components is equally important and together they act as building blocks for success.

Each finance function component feeds into and supports the next. A business owner cannot have good reporting without having good data first. In the same way, he cannot refine projections without good reporting. Without good projections, it becomes more difficult to plan, let alone efficiently execute. And without a solid plan, SMB owners stand the risk of failing to attract capital or agreeing to transactions that fail to meet their needs or are not aligned with their long-term goals.

Operational and corporate finance overlap in the planning phase. SMB owners have the best potential to achieve their business goals and objectives when they understand the value of the finance function across the entire spectrum of finance capabilities. This is precisely why I have developed a **modified definition of finance**: *The vein that connects teams with data and companies with capital.* Before we can further explore this idea, we

Modified definition of finance: The vein that connects teams with data and companies with capital.

must first appreciate the independent value of each of these five components.

Data

Data is the first component of the finance spectrum. *Data* is information that has been deemed valuable enough to capture, extract, and analyze. The sooner SMB owners identify the "right" data to capture, the better. Later we will explore how data is a fundamental component of achieving strong financial management and confident transaction execution.

In the case of the manufacturer we discussed in chapter 2, it would be wise to understand how many products can be created in a shift or what it takes to create a product from a time, labor, and equipment perspective. There are all sorts of systems and processes for the collection of data. If a type of data is important enough, I don't care how it is collected! Even if someone stands there and writes it all down by hand. The most important thing is that critical data is captured consistently. If a business owner is trying to determine demand for a product but only has a portion of the sales pipeline written down, then what good is the data? Capturing less than 100 percent of certain data can cloud the picture and be misleading, driving suboptimal decision-making.

WHAT'S AT STAKE?

Again, you can't manage what you can't measure. If business owners do not have timely, accurate information (including accounting output and all other forms of operational data) they can't confirm whether decisions are working. If an SMB owner needs to make an inventory decision about whether to stock more of product A versus product B, the numbers showing unit sales trends for each are key to predicting future inventory. A lack of data leads to finger pointing when something bad happens, whereas with the data in hand, we can have a conversation about why. For this reason, I say that *the purpose of data is dialogue*. A business owner cannot improve without assessing the outputs. It is a simple and important function, and technology has made it easier than ever to collect. So just do it!

The purpose of data is dialogue.

Reporting

Once data has been collected, the reporting process enables a business owner to harness that data. Companies can often create reams and reams of paper filled with data (we call this "reporting hell"), but the problem is that the most important data for decision making is probably only in a few pages. Reporting involves understanding how data should be analyzed and visualized in order to make it useful for team socialization and decision-making. Reporting overhauls are the number one thing private equity-backed companies seek from First Water, because owners do not want to dig for a needle in a haystack. Time spent sifting has a high opportunity cost. Reporting is an essential finance component because it creates a "line of sight" into the performance drivers of the business. A business owner cannot create good reporting without solid data capture, extraction, and analysis.

WHAT'S AT STAKE?

Having the data is not enough. You have to figure out how to harness it. Failure to understand which data is important can be more dangerous than not tracking data at all, because it can lead to decisions based on the *wrong data*. Businesses that do not report the right data will not know if their goals are being met, or even if they are feasible. As a result, there is a higher risk that targets may not be achievable, which could have disastrous consequences. Without focused reporting, we risk losing both clarity and time, and maybe the business itself.

Projections

Projections are looking forward to assess the operational and financial impact of different outcomes, both good and bad. When projections are built on top of strong reporting, business owners can further refine their projection methodologies over time by comparing actual results to prior forecasts. This component of the spectrum allows business owners to not only look forward, but to also establish credibility when communicating projections.

Understanding what items can be forecast and with what level of confidence is a core aspect of the projection component. There will always be areas that cannot be projected with high confidence (such as lumpy, one-time revenues). While not ideal, even poor projectability is manageable if a business owner realizes that *less* projectability correlates to *more* need for testing different outcomes (i.e., scenario analysis). Proper scenario analysis allows business owners to build contingency plans and understand more about the risks they face.

WHAT'S AT STAKE?

Business owners need to be able to see around the corner, not just six inches in front of their faces. Otherwise it is too easy to be taken by surprise, and this happens way too often. You can go broke if you sell less than expected, although selling much more than planned for can be equally as bad. The key point is that an inability to calculate and analyze future outcomes can be ruinous, and this includes positive outcomes! High growth situations are often harder to manage than weak sales. Though we may not be able to project everything, certain things matter more than others, for example, product demand, sales, inventory, contractual agreements, cash, etc.

Planning

Even if we can look forward, we still need to prioritize and prepare for scenarios that may differ from our projections. Simply put, planning is a series of "what if"s. There is a popular Mike Tyson saying: "Everyone has a plan until they get punched in the mouth." While business owners naturally envision themselves pursuing new opportunities, it is quite a different set of skills to understand how much money it will take, quantify the risks, and plan for the upsides and downsides.

Planning is a combination of an ROI mentality and financing alignment. A business owner with an ROI mentality sees every dollar as an investment, not an expense. The return and risk profile of various options must be defined before making a capital investment into a particular bucket. When stepping to the plate, should an owner swing for the fences or play for singles and doubles? Without planning, an owner may not even know how many strikes are left. Only businesses that utilize projection and planning capabilities can properly prepare for various outcomes and the associated financial ramifications.

The planning phase is particularly important because it is the bridge between operational finance and corporate finance. Therefore, the planning component of the spectrum is a major Relational Finance differentiator. It creates a way for operational and corporate finance to work together. The planning phase is where the growth and capital roadmaps get aligned.

WHAT'S AT STAKE?

Every business, no matter the size, only has so many dollars to invest. Wisely making investment and capital allocation decisions is critical for a business to reach its growth goals as fast as possible while mitigating risks. A business owner could decide to invest in finance processes, salespeople, a new machine, or to improve other aspects of business operations. One of the biggest reasons why investing in finance often gets de-prioritized is because owners center their attention on tangible financial ROI, such as bringing in an additional salesperson. However, failure to invest in capabilities with less immediately tangible ROI, such as finance, can result in significant downside later.

Capital

Capital is the lifeblood of a company. It feeds operations and growth. This finance spectrum component is where the growth and capital trajectory merge. Whether a business owner needs capital access to fund growth or to monetize an interest in the company (i.e., sell all or part of the business), capital access is a short- and long-term necessity. Therefore, business owners need to understand how capital providers analyze their businesses in order to maximize engagement with those providers (a.k.a., the person on the other side of the table).

Capital is the lifeblood of a company.

Critically, business owners who *only* focus on the capital component and ignore the operational finance building blocks—

including data, reporting, and projections—are at a major disadvantage. Engaging capital providers without insight into performance, a credible outlook, and the ability to define your capital needs makes for a rough dialogue.

WHAT'S AT STAKE?

The risk to capital is binary. If you run out, the game is over. We need to do whatever is necessary to make sure you have *some* (to live) and *enough* (to fund growth and other objectives) in your effort to get *more* (income, value, etc.). Recall, good surprises can be just as dangerous as bad surprises. If your capital needs are not aligned with your growth plans, you have a bad plan. To accomplish your goals, whether growth or eventual sale (or both), outside capital partners often become an integral part of the journey. Knowing how to effectively engage with the different kinds of capital partners can be the difference between success and failure. In the next chapter, we're going to dive into traditional finance models and how business owners leverage different capital providers to achieve their goals.

FROM THE FINANCE SPECTRUM TO THE GROWTH AND CAPITAL ROADMAPS

Investing in each of these five components gives business owners the right tools and processes they need to plot and navigate their path effectively. These finance spectrum capabilities are essential for successfully managing a business, pursuing growth, ensuring financing availability, and executing on transaction initiatives (including opportunistic ones).

The best way to execute on any and all future capital transactions (with the best terms possible) is to run a business as well as possible today. Business owners stand to harness the power of the full finance spectrum by understanding that the best way to do well in corporate finance is to be strong in operational finance. In doing so, they gain a serious leg up on their competition. Not only that, the path will be more fun!

The best way to execute on any and all future capital transactions (with the best terms possible) is to run a business as well as possible today.

When each component of the finance spectrum fuses together, business owners generate and align two key tools that we've mentioned before: the *growth roadmap* and the *capital roadmap*. Pairing the pathway to growth with the appropriate capital access is essential to success. When the roadmaps are aligned, there are fewer bumps along the way, and that means putting the pedal to the metal to accelerate with confidence!

The growth and capital roadmaps are tied to most business owner objectives. These may include getting bigger, reducing risk, increasing company value, making more money (higher profitability), and/or selling for maximum value. Said simply, finance capabilities provide an enormous boost for business management and transaction execution. These are the tools that help you make informed decisions with the confidence that the decisions you make today are the next step toward your long-term goals.

THE GROWTH AND CAPITAL ROADMAPS IN ACTION

Let us illustrate this concept with an example of how the finance spectrum changed the trajectory of the manufacturer from chapter 2.

The growth inflection point of the manufacturer came when a major prospective customer expressed interest in using the company, which represented an opportunity to double the current revenue. However, it was necessary to establish fully-equipped shops in two other cities to meet the local needs of the customer. How was this story resolved?

The manufacturer took the opportunity to expand and went for it (cue: cliff-jumping sound effects). Capital was secured from a bank loan and a private investor to open three new facilities and triple the production staff. Suddenly, cash was being burned faster than it could be earned and collected. Out of compliance with the bank loan, the bank refused to extend additional credit and demanded, "You've got to get a handle on this thing!" Then, the private investor questioned, "How deep is this black hole?" Our manufacturer had jumped without a parachute for the last time. Help was needed.

A business owner can have the best product or service in the world, but it does not matter if there is no funding. Businesses fail for many reasons, but the thread that ties failing businesses together is the lack of access to capital. The term "access" is critical. In order to achieve growth, businesses sometimes are willing to be less profitable or even unprofitable for a period of time. These inflection points become ugly fast as owners realize that the funding necessary for survival is just not there. Thankfully, this is not the end of story for our manufacturer friend.

He engaged a Relational Finance specialist who, as a starting point, dug into the data and financials of the company to understand the working capital nuances of the business. Together, they took control of the outlook of the business by developing better projections. Then, they presented it to the bank through the lens of a lender, showing the step-by-step process that would return the company to compliance. The result? Instant credibility. The bank agreed to continue the relationship.

I frequently share this story because business owners need to realize that the bigger the opportunity, the bigger the risk. One misstep can risk the entire company. With that said, even the worst situations can sometimes be resolved for the good, but the solution begins with putting the finance function in place. By investing in finance capabilities, our manufacturer survived and was able to get the growth and capital roadmaps back on track.

WATCH OUT FOR CINDERBLOCKS

Profitability is the ultimate lease on life for a business owner. Once a business is profitable, it can, in theory, live forever. But blindly chasing profitability can inadvertently chain a cinderblock around the ankle of a business and impede acceleration and further growth. Let me explain what I mean.

Not all growth is good growth.

Not all growth is good growth. For example, a business owner who fails to properly plan for the resources a big customer will consume risks being unable to pursue other customers. One customer may turn out to be an "opportunity cost" for many other customers. As a result, blindly chasing profitability and revenue may result in the owner catering to a single customer (if the customer is big enough). While this may not sound harmful, allowing a single customer to consume a disproportionate amount of resources can be worse than going out of business. This customer becomes the cinderblock.

Further, good growth quickly becomes bad growth when it is financed with suboptimal capital. Just as all growth is not created equal, the same is true for capital and capital partners. Even if capital enables an attractive growth opportunity now, it may not matter if it comes with nosebleed interest rates or the loss of control of the business. Once business owners commit to financing, they are locked in. Therefore, the onus is on the owner to bring the right partners to the table, and that comes through having aligned growth and capital roadmaps. The only way to quickly escape from a bad capital deal is to find another capital provider, which may not be feasible. Meanwhile, great opportunities may be passing by. The wrong capital is a particularly painful kind of cinderblock.

The growth and capital roadmaps make all the difference. Planning for growth the right way, by leveraging finance capabilities, makes executing on that growth and attracting the necessary capital much easier. With respect to capital, it is critical to become savvy about the structures and restrictions employed by different capital providers. If you are a business owner and you are ready to increase your likelihood for success, you must intimately explore the workings of traditional finance models. We are devoting this next chapter to talk about traditional finance models, their structure, their inherent conflicts, and what you need to know before entering into a relationship.

CHAPTER 4

THE LANDSCAPE OF TRADITIONAL FINANCE MODELS

To understand the need for an alternative to traditional finance models, we must first explore the models that currently exist. Traditional finance models currently provide the five components of the finance spectrum (data, reporting, projections, planning, and capital). The components in and of themselves are not new.

The problem is that, until now, these components have not collectively existed inside one model. SMB owners could hire a consultant to focus on data and reporting, but that same person would probably be unable to move those building blocks forward into the projections, planning, and capital components of the business. Of course, a business owner can engage one or more outside advisors to assist with an individual component. However, having multiple advisors involved, potentially over the course of years, presents a risk to the business because the fragmented approach hinders the ability for all the components to work synergistically toward long-term goals.

Each of the traditional finance models serve an important purpose and can provide significant value to business owners. With that said, by design, the traditional models are often difficult to access and are a minefield for SMB owners to navigate without the benefit of finance expertise. In this chapter we will explore in depth the terrain of the traditional finance models and delineate the opportunities, limitations, and inherent conflicts within each. These include short-term engagements which may not be aligned with the long-term success of the business (e.g., consultants); transaction catalysts that trigger compensation (e.g., investment banks); and transaction catalysts that are requirements in order to engage at all (e.g., private equity).

Ultimately, the business owner carries a heavy responsibility to understand available options amid the natural conflicts in order to call the shots with outside experts. Owners who crack the code can make the best possible decisions, and few things help more than having the right players on their side of the table.

THE TRADITIONAL MODEL LANDSCAPE

Because of my unique experience sitting in the seats of many of these traditional finance models, a part of what I do now at First Water is helping business owners gain insight into their counterparts on the other side of the table. The four traditional model landscapes which we will explore in this chapter are (1) project consulting and interim leaders, (2) investment banks and intermediaries, (3) bank and non-bank lenders, and (4) private equity investors.

The fact that I have devoted an entire chapter to detailing this landscape should speak volumes about how important I believe this information is for you. At the end of this chapter you will understand the purpose of each model, how the models choose to engage, how the models make their money, and the agreed terms under which the models work with a business.

Knowledge and perspective on how each traditional finance model operates is a critical piece of this story. The limitations and conflicts within these models are the drivers behind the alternative model that we are building up to in the next chapter. So, let's meet our group of experts!

Project Consulting and Interim Leaders

The first group of experts I want to explore—the only ones serving the operational finance pieces of the finance spectrum—are project consultants and interim leaders (collectively, consultants). Hiring a consultant is a business owner's way to get outside expertise around operational finance processes and capabilities without employing internal staff. As we have already learned, this is particularly relevant to data capture, reporting, and projections. A business owner may also decide to hire a consultant to implement systems, design processes, improve compensation models, or one of many other things.

Consultants typically work with a business owner over a short period of time. They come in, complete their work, transition any processes or tools to someone inside the business, and then they are gone. This puts processes into the hands of those who did not design them. Even if well-trained, what happens if the designated employee(s) leave? This represents one of the biggest challenges of consulting, and importantly, one of the biggest risks to the owner.

There is no guarantee that the tools and processes will live on after the consultants leave.

Consultants are very knowledgeable and bring an array of skills to the table, but SMB owners need to realize the onus is on them to define the way they engage with the consultant. Therefore, the business owner must be able to prioritize the functions for the consultant to act on and create value. With that in mind, if money is to be invested in a consultant, the owner better take charge of the scope and make sure the consultant adds value. If not, the work and outputs may not be aligned with the short- or long-term goals and objectives of the business. Furthermore, given the short-term nature of the engagement, consultants usually are unable to invest in the time required to understand the nuances of the business or appreciate the longer-term game plan before they start.

The best consultants will consider the context of the project in relationship to the growth and capital roadmaps, but they are still reliant on the business owner defining and communicating those roadmaps. By the very nature of their role, the vast majority of consultants want to complete the project they are assigned and then walk away. Often times, if a business owner asks a consultant to work on something that may be inefficient or unaligned, the fault and long-term results will rest on the business owner because the consultant is not there to oversee the entirety of the journey.

Consulting firms are incentivized to assign the greatest number of fully-engaged consultants for the longest period of time. The more consultants within the firm, the less flexibility they typically can offer in an individual relationship. Imagine trying to manage a thousand consultants without any consistency in hourly rates or engagement structures! In and of itself, this inflexibility is not necessarily a bad thing, but it is an important part of the consulting firm model that SMB owners need to understand.

With all this in mind, partnering with a consultant can be an excellent idea. There are plenty of situations where it makes sense to hire a consultant. The key is that the owner must be able to answer why and how to engage.

Investment Banks and Intermediaries

Let us explore the second group of experts—investments banks. This group includes other capital intermediaries, such as business brokers. For our purposes, we will focus on investment banks because many of the same things apply to other intermediaries.

There are four reasons why an SMB owner would engage with an investment bank. They are: (1) to raise capital, (2) to sell the company, (3) to execute a merger or acquisition, or (4) to engage in some sort of balance sheet activity such as a restructuring. Regardless, the primary charge to an investment bank is to complete a transaction, often with an incentive to do the largest deal possible, as quickly as possible.

There are four reasons why an SMB owner would engage with an investment bank. They are: (1) to raise capital, (2) to sell the company, (3) to execute a merger or acquisition, or (4) to engage in some sort of balance sheet activity such as a restructuring.

Some investment banks specialize in specific industries. It can be beneficial to a business owner to find a banker who knows some or all of the potential buyers, investors, and merger partners in a given space. Once an investment banker gathers the historical information of the business and understands the company, sector, and market outlook, the investment banker will act as a representative for the owner. An investment banker will put together marketing materials and a prospective capital partner list and then reach out to potential investors or buyers. Upon receiving interest, the investment banker will run a bidding processes, negotiate letters of intent, facilitate due diligence, offer guidance on negotiations, and help the owner through legal documentation to close the deal.

Understanding how an investment banker can help business owners with their goals really drives home the importance of the internal finance function components we have been discussing. Investment banks want to create marketing materials that present historical data together with future information and projections. If an owner has never previously created projections, it will be harder to convince a potential buyer that the post-transaction projections for that business are credible. With that in mind, an intermediary is going to put out the rosiest view of the future, and surely it is better if the company can substantiate a track record of building projections and meeting them.

The problem with investment banks is they only get involved with a business when the transaction process starts. They almost never get involved early enough to help the business owner adequately prepare. It is important to note that investment banks are not equipped to help the business best position itself before a sale. Instead, they prefer that owners come to them when they are ready. Again, this is not necessarily bad, it is just how the model works. Once the investment bank completes a transaction, their work is done.

For this reason, the best way for an owner to prepare for the best possible transaction is by running the business well today. All SMB owners must realize that the ability to get the most out of any transaction starts well before that first conversation with the investment banker. This is precisely why the first four components of the finance spectrum (data, reporting, projecting, planning) are critical and foundational. Investment bankers are charged with presenting the business in the best possible light. When faced with marketing an unattractive target, investment bankers will sometimes call the process "putting lipstick on the pig." The reality is nobody becomes a pig overnight. We will spend adequate time later discussing how to ensure your business is not a "pig" come deal time.

All SMB owners must realize that the ability to get the most out of any transaction starts well before that first conversation with the investment banker.

Investment banks are typically paid a monthly advisory fee and a success fee upon the closing of a transaction. Their focus, and the big dollars, is on the success fee. Investment banks therefore are incentivized for the deal to happen, whether or not it is in the best interest of the owner. The owner better be sure they want to do that deal.

There exists an inherent conflict. Let me ask you a question. If an investment banker has a success fee tied to closing a transaction and a big deal is on the table, what do you assume that banker will recommend? When a business owner hires an investment bank, the mandate to the banker is to complete a transaction.

This creates a tricky landscape for the business owner. A deal on the table does not always mean it *should* be closed. There may be wiser options such as a different deal, waiting until you can achieve better execution, or not doing a deal at all. While there are plenty of investment banks that would be respectful of an owner's decision to end the sale, the owner should not rely upon the banker to provide fully objective advice. Economic incentives are among the most powerful of incentives.

When we talk about Relational Finance in the next chapter, I will present a relationship model that mitigates these conflicts and paves the path to better transaction execution.

Banks and Non-Bank Lenders

Let us explore bank and non-bank lenders. Businesses primarily use banks for two things: debt financing and treasury management services (e.g. checking/savings accounts, credit cards, etc.). For the purposes of this book, we will bypass treasury management services, which include moving money around, processing payments from customers and to vendors, and the like. They are not unimportant, but they are about access to services rather than access to capital, which is our focus here.

Businesses use lines of credit, loans, and other credit facilities from banks and other lenders. They use this credit access to finance working capital (e.g. receivables and inventory), equipment, other purchases and acquisitions, or to optimize the amount of debt in the company's capital structure.

It is key for SMB owners to recognize that banks are very risk-averse and hyper-focused on capital preservation, i.e., limiting their downside. When a bank makes a loan, their upside is capped (or fixed) on the day they make the loan. They can only get back the face amount of the loan (also referred to as the "principal" or "par value"), plus the interest on that face amount. Their potential downside, however, is much greater. The bank could lose some, or all, of the principal. For this reason, it is important for owners to understand that banks do not necessarily like or care about growth. A bank does not necessarily care what the business is worth when they make a loan, even if the business doubles in size twelve months later. The bank's upside stays the same. Similar to other traditional finance models, banks are not inside the head of the business owner with respect to long-term objectives.

For this reason, banks can be difficult to utilize for high-growth SMBs because they cannot keep up with the business story. Instead, banks only look at financial statements and primarily lend based on historical performance. If, suddenly, an owner acquires ten big customers that triple business performance on a forward-looking basis, the banks usually are not ready (or willing) to make the effort to understand whether or not it is a valid financial story. It just has not yet appeared in the historical financial numbers. When it does, they may be happy to open the credit spigot, but that may be well after you needed the capital.

Because banks have capped upside potential, they place a lot of restrictions on business owners when they make loans. Again, this is not necessarily a negative of the model. It is only the reality of this kind of capital. If the bank tells a business owner they will lend up to two times *EBITDA* (earnings before interest, taxes, depreciation, and amortization—a key cash flow proxy and business valuation metric), the owner must ensure that EBITDA remains above a certain threshold in order to stay compliant. If you aren't familiar with EBITDA, don't worry and press on. We will explore this in more depth in chapter 6. Other examples of restrictions include how much can be invested in equipment, whether the business can get other financing, even how much of the profits can be distributed to owners.

Owners need to operate in a way that stays within their covenants—such as leverage multiples and debt service coverage ratios—in order to stay compliant. As you likely deduced, debt covenants can restrict business growth by prohibiting certain activities or investments that would otherwise be sound business decisions, even no-brainers. Even worse, violating a covenant is a default under the loan agreement, and banks may elect to take control of, or even liquidate, the business as a result of this default to recover their outstanding loan balance.

The primary way banks make their money is through *net interest margin*—the difference between the interest rate on loans made and the rate paid out to the bank's depositors (whose deposits are used to make the loans). For example, a bank that makes loans at 7 percent and pays its depositors 2 percent has a net interest margin of 5 percent. This is a simplified way of how this works given regulations and risk capital holds, but nonetheless is helpful to understand when dealing with banks. If they have deposits, they want to make loans.

Non-bank lenders fill the gap between bank loans and equity investors. Non-bank debt often has higher interest rates, though as the trade-off it may be available at higher total leverage and with more flexible structures because it does not fall under restrictive bank regulations. Plus, since it is debt, it does not dilute the equity ownership of the business (save for debt instruments that have equity-linked features such as convertible notes or warrants). There are a number of different types of non-bank lenders: hedge funds, mezzanine lenders, direct lending funds, small business investment companies (SBICs), and business development companies (BDCs), among others.

As an aside, only the best bankers will direct an owner to another lender if better execution would be available from another capital provider. I have a banker friend who knows her bank is suboptimal at mortgages. Therefore, she will say to her clients, "Hey, we want to be your banker, finance your business, and hold your deposits. But you know what? We're really not great at mortgages. Let me refer you to somebody who I know that will do a good job for you on that piece."

So how will a business owner know if bank financing is the right financing for the situation? The only way to know is to have a handle on the growth and capital roadmaps—a product of having the finance spectrum components firing on all cylinders.

Private Equity Firms and Other Equity Investors

Private equity firms possess a great deal of financial knowledge to offer SMB owners and are experts at mergers and acquisitions (M&A). Private equity firms raise capital into fund pools, and they are responsible for investing and managing those funds. They go out into the market looking for business owners who either need growth capital or who desire to sell their companies. Owners must understand that capital is *the* catalyst for engagement with this model. All a business owner will receive before they do a deal are promises that a private equity firm, or other equity investors, will work with them to do great things. Many will deliver, but not all. It is difficult to build a trusting relationship when capital (and often a controlling stake in the business) has to change hands first!

Unlike banks, private equity firms seek upside in their investments, so they focus more on the growth story and growth potential of companies. Of course, they still care very much about not losing money, but they are more incentivized to be focused on growth rather than capital preservation. Private equity firms make their money through management and performance fees. As the name implies, management fees are charged as a percent of the assets that they manage in their funds. Performance fees (also known as "carried interest" or "promote") are charged as a percentage of the profits earned on investments. The most common fee structure is "2 and 20", which means a 2 percent management fee and a 20 percent performance fee. Because of the upside they seek, private equity firms have a "buy low, sell high" mentality, meaning they prefer to pay the lowest price they can when acquiring a company.

Private equity funds also want to control the timing of the monetization of their investments since their funds have specified time horizons. A traditional private equity fund might have a life of eight to ten years. Therefore, if a firm makes an investment in a company in year four of that fund, they are looking for an exit within the next few years. Business owners who consider deals with private equity firms must understand the clock is ticking once the transaction is completed. The targeted timing of the exit may or may not be aligned with a business owner's objectives. Owners need to be confident that this type of capital and partner are the right fit for them.

Owners need to be confident that the type of capital and partner, including the investment horizon, are the right fit for them.

A private equity firm sitting across the table from a business owner wants and needs to deploy its capital. If the private equity firm likes the company, they will try to convince the business owner that a transaction now is the answer, and that they are the best partner. It is certainly possible that the way they invest, structure, control, etc., aligns perfectly with a business owner's growth roadmap, capital roadmap, and monetization objectives. However, it may not. Private equity firms are incentivized to fit good businesses into their model, even if there is potentially a better solution out there for the seller.

This is the inherent conflict within this model, and owners must be aware of this perspective from the beginning. Once again, the onus is on the owner to understand all of this. Of all the models, private equity is the most sophisticated when it comes to transactions and capital structuring. This is the benefit of having them involved with your company, but also the downside of negotiating with them on the front end. The contrast between their experience and that of the typical SMB owner is stark. Most SMB owners have never been through a private equity transaction before.

Private equity is contractually obligated to its limited partners to deploy and manage capital. In layman's terms, if a private equity firm were to help a business owner in a company in which it did not have an investment, the private equity firm would be violating its duty to its investors. As you can imagine, investors would become enraged if they were paying private equity lots of money to invest and manage the money, and they were doing anything other than that. Therefore, private equity is not going to help a business owner unless they own the company first.

From a governance perspective, institutional capital will restrict or control a business in ways never before experienced. Control can be a tricky concept, and can have a variety of degrees depending on whether a business owner sells 30 percent, 80 percent, or 100 percent of the company. Control, or governance, is negotiated, so it cannot be assumed to be one thing or another simply based on the percentage of the company owned.

Either way, a business owner should always expect that this money will have some serious strings attached. That is, the owner no longer has *carte blanche* with respect to the business and its finances. Even if it is reasonable and fair, it can still be a bitter pill to swallow for anyone who has run a business for many years without these restrictions. This is the reality of partnering with private equity, and businesses owners are better prepared by knowing this before they take the plunge.

WHERE TO GO FROM HERE?

Now that you better understand the opportunities and limitations within traditional finance models, we can really dig into the question, "Where to go from here?"

Again, I am not suggesting that any of these traditional finance models are good or bad. They all play a productive and valuable role in the market. Instead, I am suggesting that the timelines and rigid frameworks of traditional finance models are designed for their own scalability and business models, and thus not solely for the SMBs they serve or to whom they provide capital.

You may wonder, "How does a business gain the knowledge to engage with all of these different models? Where do I start?"

These were the very same questions I asked myself at the beginning of my journey. I felt passionate about unlocking the expertise and secrets that have been hidden away inside these traditional models. I wanted to explore whether there was a way to remove upfront transaction requirements for SMBs to gain access. Importantly, I wanted to use all this knowledge to champion the advancement of SMBs in a cost-effective way which would allow them to invest earlier in their finance function to grow faster, reduce risk, and get the most out of their transactions.

The answer to these questions is Relational Finance. Everything we have discussed has led us to the most important part of this book.

CHAPTER 5

THE RELATIONAL FINANCE MODEL

I pursued a career in finance because I wanted to create opportunities for businesses to grow and for owners to realize the value of their toils. However, early in my career, I often found that I was trying to help business owners operate within models that, while not inherently bad, were not the right fit for them. I felt the real conflict was that I had no freedom or flexibility to guide them in another direction. This was not right. I have met many great business owners who have truly inspiring stories. I wanted to help them have the best chance of achieving success.

This desire compelled me to devise a better way for all businesses to access the finance expertise they deserve, regardless of the confines of the traditional finance models. Good companies with good teams, in good (or even bad) situations, deserve to access finance capabilities in a manner that is cost effective, flexible, and aligned. Conversations about finance should always start, and remain centered, around the goals of the business owner.

Good companies with good teams, in good (or even bad) situations, deserve to access finance capabilities in a manner that is cost effective, flexible, and aligned. Conversations about finance should always start, and remain centered, around the goals of the business owner.

From where I stood, I believed the market was in the early stage of shifting to the advantage of SMB owners. However, with increased opportunity comes increased risk and competition. If you are a business owner, you have seen how every market has become even more competitive. This is largely because it is now easier than ever to start a business. Thanks to the internet, social media, and expanded freelancer access to just about every service, the barriers to entry have been lowered in almost every industry. In particular, disruptive business models are growing faster because consumers are increasingly demanding, and capital is readily available to fund efforts to displace legacy business models.

In this competitive market, businesses must take advantage of every opportunity to differentiate themselves from the competition, and one of those areas is certainly finance. Companies who ramp up their finance capabilities get a leg up on their peers who lack knowledge about the finance function and who get tripped up as a result. In this environment, doing nothing is not an adequate plan. If those around you are accelerating, then being in neutral is the same as falling behind. Business leaders who understand and prioritize finance can access a different gear to set themselves apart.

Another important shift that has been taking place is the abundance of available capital. Twenty or thirty years ago, the number of good companies far exceeded the amount of capital available in the market. Today the roles are reversed. Private equity funds sit on nearly a trillion dollars that need to be deployed. In spite of this shift, investors and companies still do not connect as easily as they should because of the private equity model. Furthermore, the majority of SMBs are not set up to be attractive to this type of investment capital. As unfortunate as this is, it creates a major competitive advantage for business owners who increase their understanding of finance and use it to gain access. They will have an abundance of suitors!

In this environment, doing nothing is not an adequate plan. If those around you are accelerating, then being in neutral is the same as falling behind. Business leaders who understand and prioritize finance can access a different gear to set themselves apart.

Based on these market observations, now is the time for SMB owners to get ahead of the competition. The market is ripe. Now is the time for businesses to invest in finance. Until now, business owners were forced to wait until they grew large enough to hire in-house finance expertise, or work within the confines of the traditional finance models. These were the only options, but now there is another way.

THE OPTIMAL WAY TO ACCESS FINANCE EXPERTISE

Now that we have highlighted the value of the finance function for growing SMBs, we are prepared to discuss the way SMBs can achieve flexible, cost effective, and aligned access to the finance expertise they deserve.

Everything we have previously talked about has led us to this revolutionary new idea called Relational Finance. Relational Finance is the solution I have designed to be the best way for SMBs to access finance expertise. Relational Finance is customized access to all five finance components, delivered through an engagement framework that promotes alignment of interests between company and advisor.

Relational Finance is customized access to all five finance components, delivered through an engagement framework that promotes alignment of interests between company and advisor.

When I designed the Relational Finance framework there were two core philosophies. First and foremost, I believe that *putting relationships before numbers yields better numbers.* Relational Finance takes into consideration that adding value is the key to building trust. Relational Finance adds value by listening to goals and helping business owners assess all of their available options. Unlike the rigid engagement frameworks of traditional models, Relational Finance has the flexibility to put the objectives of the business owner first, treating the finance spectrum and the relationship structure as a toolbox to craft optimal solutions. *Relational Finance provides perspective without conflict since it is not tied to any specific finance model at the inception of the relationship.* Relational Finance has the freedom to identify all available solutions, the skills to deliver on the chosen solution, and the flexibility to design an engagement model to fit that objective. Relational Finance can tailor its engagement to fit the needs of the business owner every time and no other finance model can offer as much.

Relational Finance provides perspective without conflict since it is not tied to any specific finance model at the inception of the relationship.

Relational Finance takes into consideration that goals may change for both good and bad reasons. From new market opportunities to a key person becoming ill, a lot of things happen in real life that change what a business owner wants or needs, as well as the required or preferred timing. With that in mind, Relational Finance focuses on structuring relationships that are flexible and promote the closest possible alignment of interests. Business owners who operate under the Relational Finance model have the flexibility to pivot, adapt, and evolve the relationship over time as their business and opportunities change. By putting the business owner first, Relational Finance structures relationships that result in better business and economic outcomes for everyone.

The second core philosophy states that *the best way to execute on future transactions (planned or opportunistic) is to run a company as well as possible today*. Even when a business owner believes a transaction is the immediate or primary objective, Relational Finance maintains a focus on the quality of the company's internal finance function. Relational Finance shows business owners how critical the finance function is to the execution of transaction initiatives. It also seeks to show business owners that, regardless of short- and long-term objectives, there is no downside to running a company well. By focusing the foundation of Relational Finance on the operational finance components of the finance spectrum, options are left open that can actually position the company to take advantage of opportunities that it otherwise would not be able to consider. Ultimately, Relational Finance is about leveraging finance capabilities for team engagement, business growth, and transaction execution.

With this focus, Relational Finance shows business owners that if they ever want to bring in outside capital for growth or sale, credibility will be one of the most important components of the transaction. Businesses must be able to show why investors and/or partners should trust their numbers, leadership, and growth story. Capital partners expect owners to be able to communicate why the partner's capital is a good match for the company's growth roadmap. In this way, Relational Finance prepares business owners to communicate their value proposition and growth roadmap. It is structured around helping owners build credibility by dissecting past performance and clearly communicating visibility into their future.

Relational Finance provides a way for outside finance expertise to join the business owner along the whole of the journey, driving confident decisions today that are aligned with both short- and long-term goals. The best positioned companies are the ones that are always ready to take advantage of opportunities (including transactions) because they run their companies well, have access to capital, and are therefore ready to pounce.

RELATIONAL FINANCE IN ACTION

The Relational Finance approach forms relationships through "we" conversations. In my firm, we do not have clients. We have partner companies. One benefit of Relational Finance is the "ownership mentality" we bring to partner companies, regardless of the nature of our relationship. Even if we are not technically a partner in the business, we make sure we act like one.

In order to illustrate how Relational Finance brings unique value to business owners, I will provide an example of how we (1) listened and tailored the best approach to add value, (2) utilized the full finance spectrum, and (3) positioned the company for future success.

It was fall 2014 when I met the owner of an inspection services company operating in the oil and gas sector. He had only been in business for three years, had grown rapidly, and recently discovered that several of his competitors were marketing themselves to private equity buyers. Unlike his competitors, the owner had no interest in selling his business and wondered if it made sense to buy one or more of his competitors. He had not explored mergers and acquisitions (M&A) as a business strategy yet, and had no prior M&A experience. This inflection point became the catalyst to engage First Water to determine a strategy, the best path forward, and to raise capital if an attractive acquisition opportunity was identified.

Almost immediately after becoming a partner company of First Water, the price of oil went into a free fall, falling from $120 a barrel to $20 in about six months. This seismic market shift changed the owner's priorities and the business found itself in the middle of a maelstrom. Customer volume started declining, customers were going out of business, and suddenly an acquisition was the farthest thought away.

As a result of the one-stop shop finance capabilities embedded within the Relational Finance model, we were able to shift gears by switching our focus areas away from those anticipated at the inception of the relationship. First Water showed this partner company how we could begin digging into labor metrics including profitability at the office and customer level. We helped implement a cash and liquidity projection process to understand what would happen to the business if sales fell further and customers paid invoices more slowly (or not at all).

Things went from bad to worse as the bank cut the company's credit line in half solely because of market volatility—not because his company violated any terms. They saw the sector risk and decided they needed to protect themselves. This is unfortunately common, because credit access tends to dry up when you need it most!

Together, we pushed forward quickly. We closed offices, let people go, dismantled infrastructure, stretched payables, and even fired unprofitable customers. We moved to a new receivables financing line away from the bank to ensure we could access liquidity, even though it was much more expensive. In the worst of times, the revenue of the company fell by 85 percent, peak to trough. And we survived!

Had we waited only two months longer to take action, the company would have folded. Had we not implemented the cash forecasting capabilities and analyzed the worst-case scenarios, or if we delayed action hoping the market would snap back, things would have gone much differently.

The following two years were painful, but we made the most out of them. We got smarter with our data, optimized labor deployment at customer sites, and leveraged our cash projection capabilities to figure out when we could release our cost-slash mind-set and return to a growth mind-set. We improved the product offering which allowed us to target new customer segments that offered stickier relationships and higher margins. In time, recovery turned into flourishing.

This business owner's relationship with my firm was able to continue because the Relational Finance model was flexible enough

of killing the business by trying to embark on the desired speed of growth without capital support.

I share these examples to illustrate that every situation is not only different, but also that these opportunities are heavily influenced by personal preferences and risk tolerances. These preferences should be explored as much as the available options. The discovery phase helps business owners not only make decisions about the next steps, but *confident* decisions. We accomplish this by not locking our partner companies into a framework before they even walk in the door. We spend time to understand our partner companies' opportunities, goals, and preferences first. Only then do we craft solutions. This runs contrary to traditional project consulting, where a scope is agreed upon before a consultant starts doing the work. Absent discovery, the risk is exponentially higher that the initial scope and related expectations will fracture once the real work begins.

The second phase of discovery is to craft a view of the process in terms of time, bandwidth, and cost. This is the collaboration and determination of the best way for the partner company and First Water to work together.

Part of the output of discovery is establishing the scope for the next stage. Consulting models try to accomplish this before they dig in. A tenet of Relational Finance is that it is impossible to truly understand objectives and have aligned interests without first spending time inside the business. This investment of time and effort is also why transaction-driven, traditional finance models undertake little time, if any, in a discovery phase. Instead, traditional models' dialogue with business owners is, "Call us when you figure it out!" That is fine and dandy, but the Relational Finance model believes owners should have someone who can help them work through their options so they can make more confident decisions. The right answer may very well be to pick up the phone and engage with that traditional intermediary or consulting firm, but not until the business owner knows why, knows how, and knows time won't be wasted barking up the wrong tree.

Discovery can be an important period for the business owner. I just started working with a new company that has two owners, both of retirement age. They have been in business for over twenty years, and in the last year they tapped into a new distribution channel that drastically changed the growth trajectory of their business. One of the business owners is ready to retire and do other things. The other owner is all in on the new growth channel and the ramifications for his personal wealth, but still wants to plot the path to retirement. Collectively, we sat down to hash out this situation. Then, based on our view of the opportunity and "getting under the hood" to better understand their company, we helped identify each owner's roadmap and identify what capital or transaction solutions are a fit. Relational Finance sometimes involves a "referee" role when there is more than one owner and each with different objectives. Through this model, we can help them work their way toward a solution that addresses all partners' objectives and moves the business forward accordingly. This builds a lot of trust and confidence with the partners if they believe their Relational Finance specialist is aligned with what they are each trying to accomplish, and that the Relational Finance partner can help them execute their chosen paths at the end of discovery.

One of the best things about Relational Finance is that we always have the flexibility and opportunity to structure our relationship in the way we believe works best, both now and in the long run. It is during discovery that we figure out the right relationship structure for each new partner company. Sometimes, the engagement model that we select as the best fit looks just like one of the traditional models, but only *after* the discovery phase is complete. The Relational Finance model approach can work with these businesses the same way the traditional models do. The biggest difference is that our partner companies vet their options and have the flexibility to pivot over time with one-stop shop access to the finance spectrum.

When executed correctly, Relational Finance is a win-win for everyone involved!

Advisory

During the advisory phase, the Relational Finance model is focused on execution. This is where First Water and the partner company execute on initiatives laid out during the discovery phase. This phase is geared around our two core service offerings: finance function transformation and capital solutions. Note that I could just as easily say operational and corporate finance.

Many times, the Relational Finance specialist is the only senior finance resource in a company, or at the very least, has the most expertise in certain areas. Because finance decisions become intertwined in many areas throughout the business, the Relational Finance specialist can become embedded into all meaningful decision-making processes and conversations. Often, this specialist is the primary point of contact for banking and investor relationships. This is beneficial for the partner company because the Relational Finance specialist is in the best position to talk with banks and investors in their language, tailored to their analytical perspective regarding their capital. This frees business owners to spend time on their specific strengths such as sales, improving operations, and developing new products.

The flexibility of the model really comes through in this phase. Until the Relational Finance specialist understands the goals of the business and the work required, it is difficult to structure an advisory agreement. The Relational Finance specialist can show a business owner that together they can do many things inside the business to the extent that there is a mutual desire and an aligned compensation framework to support it. In the course of developing, maintaining, and growing a long-term relationship, the Relational Finance specialist may have periods of more or less involvement. This is ultimately a great benefit to business owners, especially when all hands on deck are needed for an unexpected and exciting opportunity!

While multiple compensation methods can be used, First Water consistently elects to work on a retained advisory basis (as compared to an hourly fee structure, for example). The retained advisory structure ensures that we are sufficiently available to partner companies. Nothing would pain me more than meeting a CEO for a round of golf, talking business the entire time, and then handing over a bill for four hours as we walk off the 18th green. That just doesn't work for me.

Relational Finance has the ability to create long lasting partnerships built around goals where success can be shared. With this type of structure, the bigger the win for the partner company, the bigger the win for the Relational Finance specialist.

Transactions and Partnerships

The third and final way in which the Relational Finance engagement model works is through transactions and partnerships. Sometimes, there are misunderstandings about what a "transaction" includes. While often thought of as simply a sale, transactions refer to accessing the capital a company needs to fund operations, fund growth, and monetize value for owners. Outside of a full sale of the business to a third party, the beauty of transaction activity within the Relational Finance model is that capital (either through capital structure clean up or new growth capital) unlocks the next growth phase of the company. In this way, capital has the potential to be more fuel for the relationship, not the culmination of the relationship. Thereafter, the Relational Finance specialist can transition seamlessly from the capital raising process to supporting the next stage of growth, where there are often additional finance function initiatives to focus on.

Because First Water has the complete finance toolbox at its disposal, there are always ways to continue to add value. We take partner companies through every step of the capital raising process, and then once they raise that capital, we can roll up our sleeves and work with them on investing that new capital in the best way possible. In fact, with new capital, the pressure is often greater than before, as businesses are expected to invest wisely and show progress to their investors.

Transactions and partnerships are one way for a Relational Finance provider to directly participate in value creation and monetization. We want our economics to be aligned with the goals and positive outcomes of our partner companies. We have the flexibility to structure to the right solution. Sometimes, we are offered the opportunity to become a partner in a business, irrespective of any individual transaction. We have found this can be one way to eradicate the inherent conflict of intermediaries. In every example where this is the case, partner companies ask First Water to be a partner because they trust we will act in their best interest for long-term goals, regardless of whether that means the biggest opportunity on the table today.

The role a Relational Finance specialist plays in a transaction can be defined in three different ways: (1) an advisor who guides the partner company through a transaction process, (2) a capital introduction intermediary who introduces partner companies to prospective capital partners who fit the mold, or (3) an investor or sponsor of an investment into the partner company. Relational Finance brings all those capabilities under one umbrella and, regardless of how they participate, Relational Finance specialists have the flexibility to play the best and preferred role in any transaction.

As an example, there is a new company with whom First Water has started working. The owner is considering selling the company, that is, if the market will support the owner's desired price. If so, a formal transaction process will be launched. If not, then we will advise the owner to focus on ways to increase the business valuation so there is greater likelihood of hitting the target. Among other factors, this may simply include the business owner running the business longer before selling. Occasionally the "right answer" is to wait on a transaction and that's not a negative. The Relational Finance model enables value enhancement initiatives during the waiting period, adding value now while still keeping the transaction in mind. The deal can then be executed at the right time and with the best terms.

There comes a point when a business owner receives an offer, or hopefully multiple ones, and a decision must be made about how to proceed. A Relational Finance specialist helps business owners navigate different structures and offers. This includes helping business owners decipher terms and alternative paths so they can confidently decide to "hit the bid" or move on to a different option.

WHY DOES RELATIONAL FINANCE WORK?

Relational Finance not only works, it is the optimal way for SMBs to access the finance expertise they deserve. Over and over again, I have proven that by getting relationships right and sharing these types of mutual successes with business owners, something pretty special happens.

The Relational Finance model operates from a place where everything does not have to be defined upfront. The model allocates time to thoroughly dig into owner goals and the business's strengths and weaknesses. It understands business owners should not have to give up control as a prerequisite for accessing finance expertise.

Change is constant in business. The flexibility to pivot focus areas and the terms of engagement as market conditions or owner preferences change is an incredibly valuable piece of the Relational Finance model.

The combination of all of these things is what distinguishes Relational Finance and makes it mutually rewarding. In 2010, I saw an opportunity for change. I wanted to create something that possessed the power to be revolutionary. Relational Finance is it. It has become the ideal way for SMBs to harness finance capabilities to grow, access capital, and transact.

RELATIONAL FINANCE: SUPERCHARGED!

Before starting First Water, I had been a private equity investor, an investment banker, a lender, and a consultant. Through Relational Finance, I bring all of these different perspectives to the partner company's side of the table. My unique institutional experience enables me to share how these perspectives (both buyer and lender) look at businesses. Consequently, the partner companies who work with my firm receive access to this expertise without other upfront requirements, such as giving up control of the company.

First Water is designed to take maximum advantage of the Relational Finance approach. Whether it is infrastructure, such as a broker-dealer affiliation for compliance around securities transactions, or the network of capital providers with whom I have worked over the last decade, every investment we make into the business improves the way we work with partner companies. This is true even when those investments mirror the capabilities of traditional finance models!

CHAPTER 6

THE POWERFUL LINK BETWEEN TEAMS, GROWTH, AND DEALS

As you've learned, finance is a fabric woven into every single function of a business. Every major decision within a company has a direct or indirect financial ramification. We have spoken about what the finance function is and why it is important. This chapter marks an important shift as we will now discuss how to put the finance function into action in three specific ways. SMBs experience the benefits of the finance function through better teams, better growth, and better deals.

Before we pull back the curtain, we must first understand why teams, growth, and deals are so significant. In order to leverage and harness the power of the finance function, SMB owners must recognize the powerful interconnection between these three key areas. Let us begin by taking a broad view of teams, growth, and deals, and draw some conclusions about the relationships between them.

WHY BETTER TEAMS?

When I talk about finance, I start with people. This causes most people to short circuit a little bit. Too many people, not just SMB owners, believe finance is all about numbers. While partially true, numbers do not drive businesses. People do. Numbers do not tell stories. People do. People are always behind rallying the troops, securing the funding to survive and grow, creating and executing on the game plan, and proactively correcting missteps.

For this very reason, it is no coincidence that when I discuss the finance function I always start with teams. By focusing on teams, business owners acknowledge that at the core, it is still people who run a business. An aligned, engaged, and accountable team will always positively impact the growth trajectory of a business. People must therefore, without compromise, be the foundation of any business in order for that business to reach its full potential.

With this understanding, SMB owners must learn how the finance function (1) supports decisions around investing in team members; (2) gets the entire team in the same boat rowing in the same direction, while helping them understand why they are rowing in the first place; and (3) explains to the team how their rowing is being measured and determines which rowers should be celebrated and which ones need coaching.

SMB owners who use the finance function to drive better accountability and performance in their teams will ultimately have fewer roadblocks in their path to growth.

If you follow my simple analogy here, you will see that SMB owners who use the finance function to drive better accountability and performance in their teams will ultimately have fewer roadblocks in their path to growth. Furthermore, super-engaged teams who are aligned with the mission of the business will perform better and move the business forward faster. An owner does a great disservice to the business by failing to focus on people first, and misses an enormous opportunity to leverage the finance function to support the team.

WHY BETTER GROWTH?

There are similarities and overlap between managing teams and managing growth. The two exist on a continuous feedback loop. There is always new information coming from inside (team, operations, sales, etc.) and outside (customers, market, etc.) the company. It does not matter what type of business we discuss; no business owner can make a decision to grow and then not pay attention. The team must constantly evaluate if the assumptions made about projected growth are actually working. If they are not, changes are needed.

With respect to the finance function, the growth component is about setting targets, projecting, tracking, and iterating accordingly. Leaders must convey growth potential to the team through a credible roadmap and hold them accountable to that path. Similarly, leaders must be equally accountable to their teams and keep the promises they make. Once this mutual accountability is in place, teams can truly soar toward growth.

In order to pull this all together, businesses must ensure they have the capacity to deliver that growth from a financial perspective. This is where the finance spectrum bridges from trackability to projectability. We will go into detail about how the components of the finance spectrum—namely data, reporting, and projections—support the execution of a growth plan. Owners who understand these continuous feedback loops are more likely to prioritize their data capture and track it to compare against their goals. We will talk about this in more depth in chapter 8.

WHY BETTER DEALS?

If it seems obvious that the best way to prepare a business for growth is to make sure that the team is motivated and pointed in the right direction, then achieving the best deal is reliant on a solid team and execution of the growth plan. Understanding this set up and interconnectivity gives a business owner the roadmap to optimal deal execution.

When we talk about deals, it is important to acknowledge that a typical business will make many types of deals over its lifetime. One of those deals may be selling the business. While the scope of deal execution is much more than a sale, there are some important takeaways that are useful for every business owner to understand, even if there are no plans to sell. Here are three various attitudes an SMB owner might have regarding a sale.

1. "I didn't see it coming."

There is a well-known finance mantra that says business owners should always be ready to transact. While making a deal may not be on an owner's priority list, part of what I show SMB owners is that this should not matter. Every business should operate as if a deal might be on the table tomorrow. Operating from a place of readiness to transact at any time helps business owners prepare for the best and worst case scenarios. In a perfect world, every SMB owner would be prepared if a major competitor came knocking at the door and said, "Hey, I'm retiring. Do you want to buy my business?" On the flip side, sometimes transactional requirements arise from negative circumstances. Business owners need to be ready if illness or another circumstance results in a need to leave and sell the business immediately.

2. "Never say never."

Some business owners say, "I'm never selling my business. I'm passing it down to my kids." While that sounds reasonable, I challenge them to think about how this mentality may shift if someone knocked on their door tomorrow and offered them a billion dollars. I could be wrong, but I think those same owners might just change their tune. For this reason, I always say that there are no bad assets, only bad prices. Everything is for sale all the time under one major condition, the right price!

3. "I want to transact...yesterday!"

Out of the three scenarios, business owners who are fully convinced they are ready to transact sometimes concern me the most. That is because SMB owners often do not appreciate how much value can be lost in failing to adequately prepare for a transaction, and that the time to start is as far in advance of the transaction as possible. Sometimes, even when owners understand this, it still does not matter. Even with eyes wide open and leaving value on the table, they want to transact and are ready to do it now. For everyone else, I try to show owners how investing in the finance function and harnessing Relational Finance may uncover better options than selling immediately—if they have the option. The best way to get the best terms on a future transaction is to run your company well today.

Business owners who understand how to best position themselves for deals know the finance function is the key to maximizing their options, especially when all five components of the finance spectrum are firing on all cylinders. With that in mind, we will talk about how the finance function building blocks come together throughout chapters 7, 8 and 9, so keep reading to see how it all fits together.

THAT'S IT!

I recently had what I would describe as a "typical" conversation with a business owner with whom I had connected on social media. This owner, like others I talk to, did not have any finance capabilities in house. The conversation revealed a ton of growth within the business, and frustration around cash management as the team tried to hold the bull by the horns. This owner voiced the need for more equipment and wanted help figuring out how to finance growth. What was needed was a capital roadmap aligned with the defined growth roadmap. Conversations with investment banks had not progressed, as the immediate capital need was not large enough to meet the threshold for interest by most investment banks.

By now, you and I both know the downside of how traditional finance models work.

Before the owner could plot his path, he needed to take stock of his big growth opportunities. We talked about whether and how these opportunities served as stepping stones toward his long-term objectives. Also, we discussed how the growth roadmap, capital roadmap, and personal preferences needed to be taken into account when selecting the "right" kind of capital for today's growth opportunities.

The majority of deals, unless the owner is selling the business, are not synonymous with the end. Instead, deals are a part of the business journey. In the short term, this particular owner needed millions of dollars of equipment. Though an eventual sale was part of the game plan, the owner did not want to sell now and recognized there was much to do in order to position the company for the "big deal" down the road.

Value is maximized when teams execute on growth and can map out the path to additional growth. When the time comes to do the big deal, you want to be ready with a credible team, a performance track record, and a great story to tell. It is great when it all comes together. Better teams. Better growth. Better deals. It really is that simple.

UNDERSTANDING VALUE CREATION AND MONETIZATION (THE EBITDA ALTAR)

The goal of building better teams, better growth, and better deals is value creation and, ultimately, monetization.

There are many techniques for calculating business valuation, but this is not a textbook about valuation. Therefore, we will generalize the conversation around one of the more common ways value is ascribed. The most common reference metric used in business valuation we've already mentioned—EBITDA, or earnings before interest, taxes, depreciation, and amortization. This term, EBITDA, is a cash flow proxy from the operations of a business that ignores the amount of debt used to fund the business and the tax structure (e.g., a limited liability company versus a corporation).

Starting from EBITDA, the "enterprise value" of a business can be thought of as a multiple of that EBITDA. The technical definition of "enterprise value" is the market capitalization (equity value) plus debt, minority interest, and preferred shares, minus total cash and cash equivalents. In laymen's terms, enterprise value is the total value of the company available to all stakeholders (i.e., debt holders and equity shareholders).

When a business owner sells a company, the amount received is the "enterprise value" minus all other capital claims on the business, such as debt. The amount the seller receives after satisfying these claims is called the "equity value." To keep things simple, higher equity value is the objective, and higher enterprise value correlates to a higher equity value. The only time it does not correlate is when a business adds debt, and the impact of that debt ends up adding less to the enterprise value than the amount of debt. As a rule of thumb, we do not want to add debt that does not increase the value of our company by more than that additional debt!

Therefore, the goal for all business owners becomes pretty simple: maximize EBITDA and the multiple applied to it. If all a business owner ever did was focus on maximizing EBITDA and positioning for the highest multiple applied, there's a good chance that all the other pieces that contribute to value creation and the ability to monetize that value will fall into place.

When it comes to monetizing a business, we should point out that historical financial performance is used for valuation analysis, but what the business did in the past pales in comparison to the future outlook. No business owner, investor, or buyer, can eat last year's earnings. For this reason, when it comes to a sale, a business owner is selling the potential of the company to generate cash flow in the future. We will discuss this at length in chapter 9, but it is worth mentioning here so that you see the tie into the finance function via projections, planning, and the associated growth roadmap.

In order to show how EBITDA-based valuation works, let's take a look at Illustration 1. In this example, the business has $5 million of EBITDA. It has $10 million of debt. If the multiple that is applied to that business is four times EBITDA, then the whole business is worth $20 million. Therefore, if the owner sells the company for $20 million, the first $10 million will pay off the debt and the owner will net $10 million.

Illustration 1:

AMOUNT OF EBITDA	MULTIPLE APPLIED	ENTERPRISE VALUE	AMOUNT OF DEBT	EQUITY VALUE
$5 million	4x	$20 million	$10 million	$10 million

Better visibility of future success will have a direct correlation with the multiple that is applied to EBITDA. A potential buyer will pay a higher multiple for the same current level of cash flow if the business can be grown faster and/or with less risk than a comparable opportunity.

In Illustration 2, let's consider another scenario for that same business with $5 million of EBITDA and $10 million of debt. If instead the business was worth six times EBITDA, then it would be worth $30 million. The business's cash flow and debt are the same, but the multiple that was applied now means that business sells for $30 million. After paying back the same $10 million of debt, now the owner will net $20 million.

Illustration 2:

AMOUNT OF EBITDA	MULTIPLE APPLIED	ENTERPRISE VALUE	AMOUNT OF DEBT	EQUITY VALUE
$5 million	6x	$30 million	$10 million	$20 million

By increasing the multiple applied by 50 percent (that is, from a multiple of four to six), this owner *doubles* the equity value of the business (from $10 million to $20 million). Here is a helpful way to think about this. As long as the enterprise value of the business is more than the debt balance, then any increase in the EBITDA multiple will flow 100 percent to the equity value. For a business owner, that's good math!

I am not shocking you by saying improving cash flow increases value. That's pretty easy to understand. However, when business owners understand valuation in the context of a multiple applied to EBITDA, there are new wrinkles in optimally positioning the company. For many in the capital world, EBITDA is the gospel. It is almost impossible to speak to a private equity professional about a company and not talk about EBITDA. They may even have secret EBITDA tattoos under those crisp business shirts.

In Illustration 3, we take this one step further by looking at two companies that have the same EBITDA and debt balance, but vast discrepancies as it relates to their finance function and related capabilities:

- **Business A** has identified M&A opportunities. Revenue has been increasing, showing the credibility of its team and their ability to execute on their growth strategy. The business has established processes in the event something catastrophic happens to the owner or another key person. These tailwinds and risk mitigants result in a significantly higher cash flow multiple. There are a variety of factors that drive up the multiple applied to EBITDA and we will delve into some of them in chapter 9.
- On the other hand, **Business B** has significant customer concentration and revenue has been declining. It needs to change its growth strategy and implement a new team that can execute. As a result, its cash flow multiple for valuation purposes is markedly lower than Business A's.

Illustration 3:

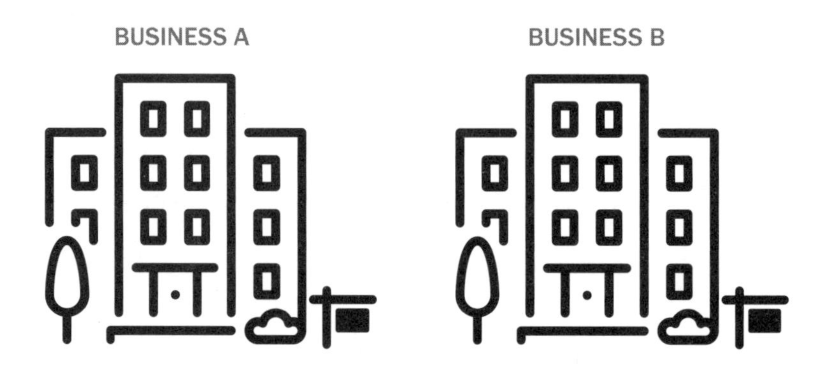

	AMOUNT OF EBITDA	MULTIPLE APPLIED	ENTERPRISE VALUE	AMOUNT OF DEBT	EQUITY VALUE
A	$8 million	6x	$48 million	$15 million	$33 million
B	$8 million	2x	$16 million	$15 million	$1 million

So, which would you rather be?

Wrap Up

Taking time to invest in this non-technical value primer was a necessary foundation to appreciate the following chapters. As we talk about the finance function and how it benefits teams, growth, and deals, it is important to translate these benefits into value creation and monetization via: (1) improvements to EBITDA, (2) the valuation multiple applied, (3) Enterprise Value, and (4) Equity Value.

Now that you understand some of the factors that impact value creation, monetization, and maximization potential, I'll show you how to put better teams, growth, and deals into practice tactically.

I want every person who reads this book to be encouraged. If you know nothing about technical valuation techniques, but focus on the factors that create value and enable monetization, the technical aspects will take care of themselves.

While business owners do not need to be valuation or deal experts, they do need to be business experts who understand the factors that contribute to value creation and monetization. Therefore, I will spend the next three chapters taking a concentrated look at how the finance function plays a critical role.

CHAPTER 7

BETTER TEAMS

While finance is intertwined with every business function, it certainly is not a business management cure-all. It cannot completely replace or make up for other important functions and roles. However, finance plays a crucial team management role that often gets overlooked. Finance can help motivate teams to rally around a mission, set targets, hold them accountable, and provide access to information that gives teams and leaders the ability to adjust or pivot.

As mentioned before, when I talk about finance, I start with people first. This perspective is key because businesses are run and led by people. In this chapter, we will look at how finance enhances and amplifies a team and the ability of the owner to lead that team. We will focus on how SMB owners tactically put their finance function into action through teams.

Having good people on a team is, of course, good. A good person might be defined as intelligent and ethical. Having the *right* person on a team, however, is even better. This person is intelligent and ethical, and has the skill set needed to fulfill a particular role. Business owners benefit from having these types of people on their team, but without the role of finance, an owner will never have the best team.

The difference between good, better, and best team members comes down to three important characteristics: alignment, engagement, and accountability. People who possess these characteristics are by far the best team members because they have a desire to apply their skills in a way that drives value creation for the business. They give their all because they (1) have the desire (they are engaged); (2) believe in the mission (they are aligned); and (3) understand what defines success for the business and themselves (they are accountable).

The difference between good, better, and best team members comes down to three important characteristics: alignment, engagement, and accountability.

The goal of this chapter is to demonstrate how finance helps create aligned, engaged, and accountable people on a business owner's team. In addition, I will review the finance capabilities an owner must possess when building and managing a team, the risks owners face without those capabilities, and the value they gain if they do it correctly.

There are three main topics that we will explore as it relates to better teams: (1) hiring, (2) goal setting and accountability, and (3) performance transparency.

The Role of Finance in Hiring Decisions

Finance is one of the key components to confident and bold decision-making, and that is no exception when it comes to hiring. Let us consider, for example, a business that has grown and is finally breaking even. It has five salespeople, but to drive continued growth the owner is contemplating doubling the sales team.

On the upside, there is a great amount of market opportunity. On the downside, there is the reality that sales professionals do not begin producing growth on the same day they walk through the door. If they did, that would make the decision a whole lot easier. Since the business is breakeven, there are no profits to reinvest. Instead the owner will need to fund the sales team ramp-up with cash, debt, or equity capital while the new hires get up to speed, familiarize themselves with products, and build customer relationships. Accepting the risk involved here, the business will become immediately unprofitable by adding the cost of the new team salaries, at least while they get ramped up. This is a necessary truth if the owner is going to pursue the incremental growth.

As a result, we must answer an important question. Can this owner afford to hire five more salespeople on a salary and commission? In order to decide, the owner needs to perform a scenario analysis that answers a series of questions which may include (but are certainly not limited to):

- What if the team knocks the ball out of the park and ramps up faster than expected?
- What if the team only produces half of the sales projected?
- What if it takes twice as long to ramp up as expected?

- What if the rest of the business performs poorly during the ramp up period?

When I talk about the role of finance in hiring, sales professionals are the easiest example because they have the most direct financial tie. If a business owner cannot project what the business will look like, how can targets be set or plans be made for what it will take to meet those targets? How does the owner set compensation for the team without anticipating the result of different scenarios on the financial health of the overall business?

Financial constraints are *real* constraints, and the risks are real. Failing to complete scenario analysis could mean a business owner risks creating a bad financial position and/or straining the relationship with new and existing team members. This is one of the many benefits of having projection capabilities.

This forward-looking mentality is more complex than thinking about what new business a sales team will bring in; it also relates to the ability of the business to operationally execute on those new opportunities. The leadership team needs to feel confident that if the salespeople meet their targets, the company can actually fill the orders! If a company cannot fill a good customer's order after the salesperson hustled to bring in the sale, both the customer and salesperson lose. This is the fastest way to lose good customers and good salespeople!

Therefore, as a business and its team continue to grow, so must the owner's knowledge about the impact of finance capabilities on hiring decisions. As I have shown here, there are many things beyond salaries to consider when hiring.

The financial risks associated with making hiring mistakes are significant. Continuing with our sales team example, owners must understand the amount of revenue their sales teams must generate in order to prevent a liquidity crunch. Payroll costs should be viewed as seriously as making debt interest payments or paying the rent each month. Each of these risks can have catastrophic ramifications for the business owner if that owner does not meet financial obligations on time. From a finance perspective, if a business owner does not have a handle on the outlook for cash, decisions about the growth and capital roadmaps are made in a vacuum. This could be a fatal mistake for the business if there is little or no margin for error.

Finance capabilities give a business owner visibility. While the owner is still responsible for making decisions, the finance function helps ensure that the resources are available to make more confident and informed decisions. As this relates to hiring or firing, no business owner sets out to hire a group of salespeople who will take months to generate business if there is a high likelihood that the business will run out of cash in that same time period. This seems like a simple concept, but in the absence of projection capabilities, how can hiring decisions be made confidently?

Adjusting for unpredictable cash flow is the reality of business ownership. This is not the case when it comes to employees who rely upon a salary every two weeks. While entrepreneurs certainly know what it is like to skip payroll in the process of growing their business, employees will not tolerate it.

Employees are not signing up for the same risks as the business owner. Likewise, they do not have the same upside that comes from business ownership and likely have markedly different financial needs and priorities than the owner. Failing to meet payroll will certainly not bring stability to your team. In fact, few things drain morale from a team more than a missed paycheck.

The myriad of risks involved in hiring decisions can be effectively addressed through finance capabilities, particularly projections. A thorough assessment leads to confident decision-making and provides the foundation for an engaged, aligned and accountable team. Finance should be one of the tools in the toolbox of every owner to limit the impact of negative surprises and position the team for success.

INVESTING VERSUS SPENDING

Traditionally, accounting functions have always viewed the people inside a business team as expenses rather than investments. There is no "people" category in the asset section of the balance sheet. There is something fundamentally not right about that. Why do people only hit the income statement as a payroll expense? How many businesses exist where the true "assets" go up and down the elevator every day?

Business owners need to view the people on their team as investments.

Business owners need to view the people on their team as investments. This shift in mentality immediately changes the expectations surrounding the team. The word investment implies an expectation of return. Just as an owner would expect a return of production and profitability on a new piece of equipment, the same is true for people. And why not?

Incorporating an ROI mentality into hiring decisions serves as the foundation for a business owner's confidence around those decisions.

Thinking about people as an investment rather than an expense requires that an owner develop an opinion about the perceived value that a team member brings into the business. It would be nonsense to hire someone for $80,000 a year and not expect at least that much value in return. Ideally, if that team member is engaged, aligned, and accountable, he or she will hopefully provide a return that is a multiple of the amount invested!

Of course, ROI is not always readily determined. A sales team will have quantifiable financial metrics that make the ROI calculation more concrete. Hiring a human resources leader, on the other hand, is much more difficult to quantify. Therefore, owners must be careful not to dismiss roles where the value is more difficult to define. The salary of a human resources team member may appear to be more like an $80,000 a year expense, but if the business owner is not compliant with labor laws, that owner is vulnerable to potentially millions of dollars in losses. For that reason, there is still the ability to apply an ROI mentality to non-production focused roles. The ability to properly assess the ROI of a team member provides a structure to hiring (and firing) decisions based on overall business and value creation objectives. If an owner is not trying to grow, or has no capacity to fill additional orders, will that owner receive an acceptable ROI on more salespeople?

A business that employs an ROI mentality also prioritizes its investments. All businesses have a finite number of dollars, and a number of ways to invest those dollars. How a business owner decides to allocate those finite resources is critical. Comparing individual investment opportunities versus others (also known as assessing opportunity cost) is a necessary step for the decision-making process. The finance term for this process is the "capital allocation methodology" of the business.

If a business owner is seeking to hire someone to drive value in the business, then it is helpful to understand what those values drivers are. A business owner may need an account manager and a salesperson, but financially is only in a position to choose one of them. How does the business owner decide which one to choose, particularly when cost is equal? Answering that question requires the owner to consider what is to gain or lose by investing in customer service versus new business. Having a rigorous ROI mentality across the business helps prioritize needs in the building of the team.

Systems and data can support a business owner in this effort, but they cannot provide the critical analysis needed to make the best decisions. Data alone will not provide the insight into whether a business owner should spend $50,000 or $100,000 on a new team member. A Relational Finance specialist can act as a strategic sounding board to incorporate that ROI framework into these important decisions.

Relational Finance specialists are in tune with the long-term value drivers of a business and can help creatively structure incentives for a team that are specifically aligned with those drivers. Such efforts are about building accountability into the growth and capital roadmaps. It is a good thing when the team is compensated around the metrics that also drive value creation for the business owner. That's real alignment!

GOAL SETTING AND ACCOUNTABILITY

Consider a manufacturing business that has five salespeople. The business owner may set a goal for each salesperson to sell $10 million of product. If they each hit this goal, the business can expect $50 million in revenue. This business owner would be in big trouble if annual production capacity is only $30 million! This is an overly simplified example meant to highlight risks associated with your team hitting targets that cannot be executed.

The way to avoid finding yourself in this situation brings us back to finance. A business owner needs to be completely prepared to sufficiently support the team in reaching its goals and follow through when they do. With that in mind, when a business owner sets goals, there must also be a way to track against those goals.

If you have ever owned or operated a business, you have learned that it is hard to hold people accountable without proper goal setting. Productive goals are those which are clearly defined and viewed as achievable by the team. That does not mean goals cannot be aggressive. Aggressive goals can be great for growth, although the onus is on the owner to anchor such goals in reality and clearly communicate expectations to individual team members. Only by doing this can an owner determine whether team investments are providing fair value (or more). Without defining what success looks like, there is no way to know whether a business owner has set productive goals or to determine whether results achieved are positive or negative.

Goal setting is both an art and a science. From a quantifiable analysis perspective, we have discussed how a business owner must tie goals back to ROI. A business owner must know without question that the goals set are directly correlated to the value expected from each team member. Here we are talking about concrete and measurable objectives.

From a more personal, subjective perspective, establishing the level of a team's goals is also a bit of an art. A business owner must realize the impact, particularly on human behavior, of choosing the level of aggressiveness or conservatism in team goals. Setting unrealistic goals (or that the team believes are unachievable) is one of the worst things for team morale. The engagement switch will quickly turn off. It is a delicate balance with an idiosyncratic understanding that varies for every business owner and team.

Accountability is a two-way street. A business owner needs to hold team members accountable to make sure they are executing on their individual tasks to fulfill the bigger vision. In the same way, team members need to hold the business owner accountable. If a team member delivers a great deal of value to the business, then that team member is going to expect that value was properly measured and manifests in incentives. This is how teams are galvanized and must be nurtured to stay aligned, engaged, and accountable. Without aligned incentives and mutual accountability, business owners run the risk of creating a fragmented, or even mutinous, team. Mutinies show that something of real value is at stake and is usually fixable, but it can have scarring effects and you would obviously prefer to avoid it if possible.

In order to get it right, business owners must realize that there is a synergistic relationship between goal setting and accountability. Proper goal setting is always a prerequisite for achieving accountability and should always tie back into the ROI framework. By understanding and properly defining each of these factors, a business owner can best determine what team members need to accomplish and how the business should compensate them. This cannot be accomplished without core finance capabilities.

NOT ALL DATA IS CREATED EQUAL

I worked with a large family-owned business, and across all of their divisions (labor, customer service, sales, etc.) everybody benchmarked their performance against sales. There was just one big problem. When we came in to talk to the team, we discovered that everyone had a different definition of sales.

It turned out that there was a perfectly good reason. The salespeople were measuring gross sales. They did not believe it was fair to be penalized for returns associated with defective products. Meanwhile, the production team measured net sales to take into account defects and returns. Despite these rational differences, all of the data circulated internally only said "sales" and the nuances were not being communicated.

From a finance perspective, holding team members accountable requires business owners to track the *right* data, and then clearly define how that data will be used across the business. However, the nature of information access in an organization can lead to data that fails to tell the whole story. Therefore, business owners must be careful to "peel back the onion" and look to the level of data and detail necessary to get to the truth about performance. Referencing our sales example, only relying on the first layer (i.e. total gross sales) without drilling down can lead to (1) misleading information, (2) poor decision making, and (3) team incentives which are misaligned with real value drivers. This is where a Relational Finance specialist can help a business owner take a closer look.

To show you what I mean by this, let us consider a business with two salespeople. Each one has customers on annual contracts, similar-sized books of business, and similar account growth goals. At the start of the new calendar year, each salesperson is charged with growing their existing accounts as well as acquiring new accounts. However, their compensation is only benchmarked against the actual revenue they generate in a year. Let's take a look at these two salespeople.

SALESPERSON A	SALESPERSON B
• Serves a couple of large accounts that have been on contracts for many years • Already knows they plan to renew • One of the larger accounts recently acquired another business and the size of this relationship has doubled • Since compensation is benchmarked off total revenue, Salesperson A realizes annual targets have already been achieved • Salesperson A will not be further incentivized to hunt for new business and enters into coast mode • At the end of the year, performance is rewarded with a big bonus	• Serves a number of accounts who've had problems with the product team not addressing their concerns • Already knows they plan to cancel contracts • Hustles to call all existing accounts to look for new opportunities • Signs up a number of new accounts to offset the product-related cancellations • Despite best efforts and hard work, Salesperson B misses annual total revenue goals • At the end of the year, there is no bonus and Salesperson B is considered for termination

Between these two salespeople, who would you want on your team?

While the answer may seem obvious, if the team does not have the proper data to support why revenue grew, why contracts were lost, and what the difference is between revenue in existing and new accounts, then the business leader may have no idea that Salesperson B is actually the better salesperson! With that in mind, the highest level of the data (total revenue) not only failed to tell the whole story about performance, but in this example actually told the opposite story.

While data is critically important, poor data can actually swing the pendulum the other way by demotivating a team. In the example above, the business owner unintentionally rewarded bad behavior and, worse, punished good behavior. Additionally, team members are observant and talk among themselves, so there is a good chance the chastised strong performer knew the other was underperforming and was *rewarded* for it! A strong finance function can ensure that the right data is being captured and analyzed, and that can be used to craft compensation structures that produce the desired team behavior and reward good performers.

It is unlikely that an issue like this will occur in a business with only two salespeople. It is easy for a business owner to stay in tune with a small number of customer accounts and a small sales team. However, as businesses and teams grow they reach an inflection point. What happens when two salespeople become twenty? This is a whole new ball game. Keeping that same intuitive finger on the pulse becomes more difficult, and we only have ten fingers! What happens when the larger size of the business hinders the ability of an owner to keep track of it all? Of course, a business owner could spend more time in the nitty gritty of every customer account, but is that the best use of time? Certainly not!

To achieve better growth, business owners should allocate their time to product, customer experience, strategic direction, competitors, funding, and other aspects of their business. Finance is a source of capabilities to support the scaling of a business, but the onus is on the owner to value the benefits and make the investment. In the sales team example, big finance investments may not be needed at only two salespeople, but hopefully we can agree the right time is before there are fifty salespeople. Of course, there is no single answer that fits every business, but it is hard to argue against the benefits of incremental investments in finance capabilities, processes, systems, and infrastructure. This is also where a Relational Finance specialist can add a lot of value.

As an example, we see business owners spend tens and even hundreds of thousands of dollars on customized implementations of Customer Relationship Management (CRM) systems. Their goal is to collect data that has the potential to help them run, manage, and measure their sales organizations better (bravo!). CRM systems are a great vehicle for creating an efficient and standardized process for collecting, aggregating, extracting, and analyzing data. One of the biggest reasons why they can be so expensive is because of the extreme level of customization. During implementation, a business owner must first know what data is the most valuable to capture so the system can be designed accordingly. No system, no matter how expensive or fancy, can do that for you.

Systems do not solve problems, they only solve bottlenecks.

Systems do not solve problems, they only solve bottlenecks. They also do not tell business owners what to track or why to track it. Therefore, owners need to know this prior to putting new systems in place. Instruction manuals and tutorials will never be able to tell a business owner how to best leverage the system for his or her unique business.

PERFORMANCE TRANSPARENCY

It is one thing to mandate goals, track against them, and hold team members accountable. In my experience, once targets and goals are set, performance transparency is a critical piece that business owners often fall short on communicating. In order to support their teams, business owners should give team members regular updates on their progress. Whether they are ahead or behind, the value of performance transparency makes it clear where they stand. Performance transparency is the third and final topic we will cover to help business owners create better teams.

Performance transparency is an investment in information flow. A team that has the same data that a business owner is watching will see when a key trend is out of whack. Equipped with this data, the team can proactively find an explanation and solution, hopefully before they are even asked about it. Performance transparency can be the difference between proactive and reactive teams. It focuses the team on the right questions, enabling them to bring proactive answers and solutions to others in the organization. Increasing communication and transparency cuts out a lot of extra chatter and increases productivity. This allows the team more time for higher-value activities. A culture of transparency is a win-win for everyone.

As humans, we have an innate desire to feel successful. The act of sharing information in and of itself can drive productivity gains. Let me show you what I mean by this with an example. In a manufacturing facility, the owner might ask the day shift to write production counts on the wall. When the night shift comes in and sees the volume of the day shift, all you need are a couple employees who believe (and can subsequently prove), "We can do better than that!" And then they do. Call it competition, call it human nature, call it anything you want, but this type of productivity improvement cycle can be accomplished without leadership ever having to say a word. I love this example because it shows just how human behavior is geared toward a desire to succeed, and it does not require much to trigger that desire into action.

There are numerous benefits to providing performance transparency, especially when paired with goal setting. A team that understands what the business is measuring, and how performance is tracking against those measurements, is set up for success. Teams who understand the business drivers in real time can escalate dialogue up the reporting chain faster. Owners should also ensure performance information ties back to prior communicated targets so that transparency maintains its effectiveness.

That is why I say the purpose of data is dialogue. Data, when combined with transparency, also has the potential to save business owners a tremendous amount of time. Communication will be more focused and issues are dealt with more efficiently. If trends get off track, the team proactively seeks out answers and solutions to present to leadership. Imagine being a business owner and having solutions presented to problems you did not yet know you had!

The purpose of data is dialogue.

The final key takeaway here is that data is valued differently by various stakeholders. This includes everyone from a line manager all the way up to the board of directors. Understanding the level of required detail is vital. The board cannot digest the same detail as an individual line manager in a business with one hundred line managers. Therefore, performance metrics are designed differently for each stakeholder audience. Understanding the wants and needs of each stakeholder is the key to designing good reporting processes. The more alignment on data within a business the better. For example, the board may see the summary metrics of those line managers, but it would not be efficient for them to review the whole of the detail that each of the hundred line managers review on their specific line.

That said, there are benefits to the line managers knowing that the board is tracking their performance as a group. Powerful performance alignment can be attained even when reporting is aligned among audiences. Communication and transparency are integral for every member of the team to know what success looks like. Powerful performance alignment is attained when reporting is aligned across audiences.

Now that you understand the value of finance capabilities in hiring, goal setting, accountability, and performance transparency, you are well on your way to achieving a team that is aligned, engaged, and accountable.

In the next chapter, we'll take a detailed look at better growth and its interconnectedness with better teams.

CHAPTER 8

BETTER GROWTH

Growth has a way of helping business owners achieve their goals: making more money, paying their team more, making their company more valuable, and eventually monetizing their business.

Growth represents the new, whether it is new customers, new products, new markets, etc. While we would all agree growth is good, not all growth is created equal. There are different levels of risk associated with different approaches to growth. I'll explain further what I mean by that in this chapter.

Growth can be equally (if not more) likely to kill a business than financial distress. In fact, distressed business owners sometimes have more room for negotiation than thriving businesses. If a bank is pressing a distressed business, the owner may throw the keys on the table and say, "Think you can do it better? Come on in! Otherwise I have a plan and you're better off working with me here."

A high growth business, on the other hand, would have a very different conversation. A popular adage is "growth is expensive," which refers to the need to outlay more cash for items such as inventory ahead of higher sales. A business may find difficulty in requesting flexibility from a vendor who sees firsthand that the business is ordering three times more than last year. Seeing that business success, that vendor could respond, "We love that you're growing, but we're not your bank and won't finance your growth. Call us when you can write a check."

There's a clear difference here, right? Nothing exceeds like *excess*. Growth can be bad if it is more than a business is ready to handle. A business owner who has not properly planned for growth may quickly be engulfed by product problems, angry customers, disgruntled employees, and/or cash constraints. Simply trying to "hold the bull by its horns" means that growth will take the business owner for a ride, not the other way around.

Nothing exceeds like excess. Growth can be bad if it is more than a business is ready to handle.

Business owners must parse the upside and downside to their growth trajectories. In doing so they will gain visibility into potential outcomes. The more visibility, the more confident the decision-making. High growth situations require proactive planning more than any other scenario to reduce the risk of "blowing up" after the ignition switch is flipped.

The relationship between confidence and risk is interesting. When business owners plan appropriately and analyze various outcomes, they make decisions with their eyes wide open. They are confident *because* they understand the risks being taken. However, confidence can be a risk in and of itself, as overconfidence can lead to decision-making without completing the requisite analysis. The finance function is a builder of the right kind of confidence by driving increased visibility into the business outlook.

The role of finance in achieving better growth can be attributed to three main areas: (1) proactive planning, (2) real-time tweaking and pivots, and (3) value optimization.

PROACTIVE PLANNING

I was recently asked to step into a company that provides reservoir characterization services to the oil and gas sector. The company sends trucks into the field for a number of on-site "job days" to do seismic imaging. The management team thinks about the business as the number of trucks, the number of days those trucks are on a job, and what the revenue is for each of those job days.

The company contacted First Water because their private equity owner wanted faster growth to position the company for sale. In this example, growth meant more job days. Therefore, the company built a budget with job days (and revenue) 30 percent higher from the previous year. On the surface everything looked promising, but within the assumptions was a very big problem.

When First Water started digging into the analysis, we showed them that to generate the revenue growth they were projecting, their existing trucks would have to operate above 100 percent capacity. The growth assumptions necessitated more job days than actually available. In addition, their budget had not assumed they would need any more trucks. This was a significant oversight, since each specialized truck cost in excess of $1 million and required four crew members. By the way, these are custom jobs requiring order lead time, not like going down to the local lot.

The team had developed projections without really understanding the existing capacity utilization in the core revenue-generating assets. The budget as presented was simply unattainable. The private equity firm welcomed the growth targets, but they were less than happy about the "surprise" capital requirements.

One of the ways First Water was able to help this company was by creating tools and processes to properly test assumptions. We built a dynamic operating model enabling the team to intertwine growth assumptions with asset, headcount, and capital requirements. We showed exactly how different levels of growth translated into additional truck and personnel investments, supporting a critical dialogue between the company and its private equity owner.

We also helped with scenario analysis by taking a closer look at the upside and downside of the growth effort. Scenario analysis is an important part of planning and ensures owners understand the risks and financial ramifications of their decisions. What would the cash situation look like if the company invested in additional trucks, but the new revenue did not materialize? How would debt covenant calculations change for their bank loan? Could the company support more debt to finance the trucks?

Better growth is unlocked when business leaders make decisions following a rigorous evaluation of the prospective impact on revenue, profitability, cash flow, liquidity, debt requirements, and owner/investor appetite for additional investment.

THE DANGER OF MISUNDERSTANDING GROWTH

Growth assumptions must be placed in context with existing operations and capacity. Failure to do so can lead to team and business failure. In the example above, here are some of the potential downsides:

- *The quality of the team's work could decline.* If the company tries to run at more than full capacity, the team will be stretched across too many jobs which could result in a reduction in quality.
- *The company could fail to deliver upon their promises to customers.* This is a great way to lose customers. Plus, failing to deliver on agreed terms is made even worse when companies make contractual promises to deliver.
- *Owners risk losing team engagement when a flawed growth plan has incentives and bonuses tied to it.* If the company had no way deliver on the proposed growth, any employees with incentives tied to those projections would surely be disappointed.

In the pursuit of growth, identifying any required investments is critical. Based on those capital requirements, the business owner will need to decide whether the investment is worth the risk and provides an attractive enough return. This is when the finance spectrum components begin working together. Projections and planning translate into a discussion around capital. In the truck example above, if the additional growth is unlikely to continue beyond the current period for the business, does the company really want to invest in additional trucks? They may rather prefer to rent, even if it is at a higher rate, instead of leasing or buying so that capacity does not sit latent when the short-term growth spurt rolls off.

Planning is a wasted effort without credible projections. A business owner who cannot measure asset capacity (i.e., data and reporting) will struggle to project asset capacity. Without projection capabilities, planning happens in a vacuum. Even good results can be ruined by a bad plan!

Planning is a wasted effort without credible projections.

Many business owners do not embrace data and reporting as mission critical. However, these functions are integral to developing solid projection and planning capabilities. Projecting in a way that is trackable and reportable allows a business to test the accuracy of its projections and improve its projection methodologies over time.

Another benefit of data, reporting, and projections is that they support growth through faster decision-making. When data is readily available it creates a feedback loop of measuring against projections, making changes, and tracking the results of those changes. This means businesses can identify problems or mistakes, correct them or quickly pivot in a new direction, and limit future surprises. Faster decisions and fewer surprises means more time allocated to important areas, like growth!

Projection quality boils down to how input drivers fit together in calculating the outputs. A simple example is estimated units sold and average unit selling price being multiplied to project revenue. If the drivers are not connected correctly, projections may be useless or even dangerous if major decisions are made based on a faulty approach. Garbage in, garbage out!

REAL TIME TWEAKING AND PIVOTS

A few years ago, I worked with a construction services company which built proprietary field software. This gave their customers real time visibility into projects and was innovative within the industry.

Unfortunately, the company came to realize that customers were not yet willing to pay for the innovation. Although many were interested in the new capabilities, customers could not get over the hump of paying more for the service. Even though the company had created a superior product, it could not realize the price and margin increases it initially expected. The company was at a major inflection point.

We analyzed the business and market and concluded that the best thing to do was to use the software across all customers, making it part of the core service offering. To put it simply, we gave it to customers for free. In doing so, we took a risk, but a calculated one. Even though customers were not willing to pay for the software, they realized (as we had hoped) it delivered value to them. As a result, they had better visibility into their data and grew accustomed to this new level of service. This solidified existing customer relationships in a price-sensitive industry where accounts can be quickly lost when a competitor comes in and underbids. Word spread, and the company started gaining more and more of the market with new customers who sought access to the new capabilities. There is a sales saying that it is hard to sell a steak to somebody who only wants a hamburger, but if you deliver a steak at hamburger prices you'll find plenty of takers.

Even though the original plan to sell the software had to be abandoned, or at least postponed, an alternative solution was found. Thankfully, the company had not bet the farm on their initial expectations. The willingness to adjust quickly, refocus marketing into the existing core service segment, and abandon the original target pricing model made the investment in the software well worth it.

Things could have gone very differently if the company had not been willing to pivot. Precious resources and time would have been wasted trying to sell the software at premium pricing, only to lose the first-mover advantage in the space. This is precisely why real-time tweaking and pivots are crucial.

Growth is a new frontier. As a place or phase where a company has not been before, the need for data and performance visibility is substantial. Faster and better decisions are made when quality information and insight is readily available.

Upon launching a new product or growth strategy, the immediate next step is a bevy of questions. Will the company be able to produce the product in line with initial cost and time expectations? Are the salespeople getting traction in the marketplace? If so, is it at the originally assumed price point? Ask fast, answer fast, and change fast. Those are the requirements for navigating a high-growth phase. Without the right data, reporting, and team in place, you risk spiraling out of control.

Businesses need to fail fast and often. Rarely do businesses get it right the first time. Performing real-time tweaking and pivots is the key to realizing growth potential. Data reveals what is failing (or working) and needs to be adjusted (or replicated). Again, you can't manage what you can't measure. A business owner must rely on a feedback loop of information, tweaks, and projections in order to constantly track against assumptions. This is particularly true in growth phases because businesses

Businesses need to fail fast and often. Rarely do businesses get it right the first time.

tend to become more financially and operationally stretched while chasing growth. In addition, more volume often means more moving pieces, which taxes the management team.

One of the main benefits of a reporting-projection feedback loop is the reduction in negative surprises. Unanticipated events result in "fire drills" where the team drops what they are doing to address the problem. This sort of interruption can be damaging, even if the reason for the surprise is a good event. More time spent reacting to surprises means less time to proactively work on the next steps in the business. It is hard to argue that a business owner is better served being reactive to fire drills than being proactive (which includes investing in further capabilities to avoid surprises).

Teams who harness the continuous reporting-projection feedback loop while pursuing growth are able to keep moving forward toward goals. Otherwise, they are waiting for the next alarm and strapping on the firefighting gear. Those fireman uniforms are heavy, physically and emotionally. People have capacity limits just like equipment or a facility. Failing to remember this may mean stretching, over-taxing, or burning out the most important assets of the company.

Fire drills can also push businesses into suboptimal operating circumstances. Without finance capabilities in place, owners are pushing important priorities down the totem pole. Not keeping tabs on equipment utilization, production payroll, or quality control before rushing to deliver on orders day in and day out will eventually lead to some big problems, especially when pursuing growth. This is no way to operate and is a pathway to failure.

By the very nature of growth, the business owner is in a new environment. Information flow and insight into data are hypercritical to test against assumptions. All information is good information, even if it is negative. Bad news is news nonetheless. Choosing what to do with that information, through real-time tweaking and pivots, enables the business to change its trajectory and to get back on that growth train.

VALUE OPTIMIZATION

Recently, First Water helped a high-growth staffing company get ready for a sale. They had tripled their profits in an eighteen-month timeframe. They were prospering, but the revenue from one of their offerings was lumpy and unpredictable. The unknowns around revenue timing, along with the rapid response nature of the staffing needs, made this part of the business very difficult to plan around. In contemplating an upcoming sale, inconsistent volumes made it difficult to position for a premium valuation.

To reduce the impact of negative value factors, the leadership made some very intelligent moves. They started training their customer base (for a fee) on how to prepare for and manage the types of events that required staffing solutions. They worked with them year-round to smooth out the risk of disruption. As a result, they were able to get customers to engage with the company more consistently, not just for the lumpy, high-need events. The biggest revenue and profits were still embedded in the core staffing offering, but they turned one-off customers into recurring customers. This added revenue in periods where they otherwise would have had none from those same customers, offsetting some of the costs of keeping people at the ready for when one of those high-need events occurred. That's a big win.

There are many lessons to be learned from how this company used better growth to add significant value:

- They drastically increased their future chances of earning staffing work by investing in stronger relationships with their customers through planning and training.
- They developed a differentiated service offering that set them apart from their competitors.
- They better utilized the capacity of their team by keeping them productive outside of the unpredictable customer events.
- They made it easier to manage their overhead and created a portion of steady and consistent revenue, which was helpful for projections and planning.
- They increased revenue and made it less lumpy (focusing on these recurring relationships versus chasing more one-time revenues), reducing revenue volatility and making it easier to manage working capital.
- They decreased their overall operating margin percentage (by adding lower margin revenue to the higher margin event activity), but increased overall margin dollars (higher EBITDA!).

The value-added benefits introduced by the company were astronomical. They made the company significantly more attractive for a sale. However, the business still had a problem: how to tell the best story possible about their growth to a potential buyer. Although this business had done the right things to increase growth and optimize value, it still needed to demonstrate the improvements and efficiently communicate with buyers.

First Water leveraged the company's data to authenticate the underlying business story. Harnessing data properly is critical in managing the business, developing the narrative, and positioning for a premium valuation.

There were clear financial benefits to the company making these changes. Even though they had reduced their margin percentage (often a red flag for buyers or investors), they created additional and stronger customer relationships which had more long-term potential. Their EBITDA was growing and the fact that it was happening at a lower margin was a good thing when laid out to show less lumpiness month-to-month. Because of the changes they made, the data available, and the ability to communicate the benefits they were able to sell the business at a premium multiple.

I shared this example to showcase how better growth impacts value in ways other than higher revenue and EBITDA. Increasing EBITDA is one way to increase value. However, the quality of that EBITDA, the story a business owner tells, and the credibility of the outlook also contribute to the determination of value (e.g., the multiple of EBITDA that an investor or buyer will apply to the business).

FACTORS THAT IMPACT VALUE

Business value becomes tangible when it is monetized. Knowledge of transaction processes and the way different capital partners analyze and assess a business is a powerful thing. This is the perspective that a Relational Finance specialist brings to your side of the table.

Long-term value creation should be at the forefront when planning for growth.

Long-term value creation should be at the forefront when planning for growth. This includes factors beyond the immediate financial impact, such as what the business is making and how, who the customers are, and the sustainability and repeatability of revenue.

It is vital to determine whether or not a growth plan will drive long-lasting value. Chasing near-term growth opportunities can come at the expense of future flexibility and value maximization. There are many situations where growth and value can be at odds. Let's take a look at two customer-related factors that can have a major impact.

The first factor that impacts value is the relation between reoccurring business and one-time transactions. Would you rather have a customer this year at 60 percent margins, or lock that customer into a five-year contract at 40 percent margins? While the former puts more money in your pocket this year, the latter fosters financial visibility over an extended period.

While every business, situation, and customer is different, businesses that have reoccurring revenue tend to be easier to manage, forecast, and finance. With that in mind, if value is partially determined by the repeatability of previous performance (i.e., historical cash flow or EBITDA), then reoccurring business is an incremental credibility driver for that EBITDA metric and associated valuation. As a result, businesses with reoccurring revenue are more attractive and fetch higher valuations. Even if a business sacrifices some EBITDA this year to get those contracts, it could have a higher multiple applied to that EBITDA because of the additional visibility.

Pricing and contract strategy is both an art and a science when it comes to long-term value creation. Many industries have defined product or pricing models where simply saying, "Get more recurring revenue," is not an option. While there is no one-size-fits-all answer, that does not negate the importance of these factors when planning for growth.

The second customer-related factor that impacts value is customer concentration. Growing a business and adding customers can be a long and difficult process. If a large customer comes knocking and begins ordering ten times the current inventory of the business, it appears to be a really good day. Wouldn't you agree? In one move, the business could take on a single customer that would equal over 90 percent of total sales.

On the surface, this kind of growth is amazing assuming the business can digest it. However, having a single customer dominate your customer base has its challenges. Knowing how dependent the company is on the revenue, the customer has considerable leverage over the business. This directly impacts the ability to plan and make investments in infrastructure, overhead, and people. How confident can you be in making long-term commitments if one customer can turn your business off like a light switch?

From a valuation perspective, this kind of customer concentration makes it difficult for a potential buyer to apply a big multiple on EBITDA. Moreover, the value of the business will likely have more to do with the health of the customer and its business. Major customer concentration puts some or even all value determination into someone else's hands. It can be hard feeling as if you do not control your own destiny.

There is both art and science in the consideration and management of customer concentration. As every business, every situation, every market, every sector, and every cycle may be different, the threshold where customer concentration becomes an issue will vary. It could be 90 percent of a business or it could be 10 percent.

Customer concentration is not a bad thing in and of itself. There are many businesses that serve one or more large customers and then use those relationships as a foundation to grow elsewhere. A business owner needs a plan for how the company will deal with customer concentration over time, preferably before the concentration exists. For example, acquiring a customer who accounts for 90 percent of your current business now may not be terrible if the growth roadmap is such where that same customer equals 10 percent in five years via additional growth. You can grow out of some risks, and growth is arguably the best cure for customer concentration.

A business owner needs a plan for how the company will deal with customer concentration over time, preferably before the concentration exists.

Relational Finance specialists ensure that value-oriented factors are part of growth planning. With the full spectrum of finance capabilities at their disposal, they support the business owner's decisions to pursue growth and the execution of that growth, all with an eye toward maximizing future valuation. Having a long-term mind-set incorporated into today's decisions inherently has a lot of value. This is not only for creating long-term value, but making sure the decisions made today do not put the business in a corner.

Now that you understand that achieving better growth requires a focus on value, and the myriad of factors impacting that value, let us address the third focal point of Relational Finance: better deals.

The next chapter will focus on a detailed review of how better deals are driven by preparation and positioning to make the business attractive to capital partners, and for the highest valuation possible.

CHAPTER 9

BETTER DEALS

Deals happen throughout the life cycle of a company and catalyze critical inflection points. Deals, like growth, may also be a new frontier for a business owner facing decisions and negotiations not previously experienced. The contracts underpinning transactions can also be difficult or impossible to unwind if the owner makes a mistake. Business owners must go into deals prepared, with confidence, and with eyes wide open. This is the only way to successfully traverse the stressful, risky path of deal execution. In this chapter, we will highlight how critical the finance function is when it comes to preparing for, negotiating, and executing a variety of deals.

When we talk about deals, we are talking about any agreement or transaction with a financial or capital ramification. Although this includes the selling of the business (the ultimate deal), there are many deals that occur along the journey. This includes how a business owner decides to finance operations, negotiate contracts, work with banks, take on investors, buy or lease, etc. Some of these may seem like inconsequential transactions, but each can have long-term implications for flexibility and the ability to realize and maximize value. When it comes to deals, it is not a case of "what doesn't kill you makes you stronger." Surviving a bad deal often means a business has been diverted from its preferred growth and capital roadmaps. This can set a business back years, if not permanently. We want to make sure deal inflection points accelerate us down the road and not into a ditch!

Better teams and better growth are the foundation for value creation. In terms of the metric we have linked to value, if teams and growth help a business owner increase EBITDA and the multiple that is applied, then better deals are a business owner's realization and monetization of that value. Part of my job is to help business owners understand how to monetize value in the business, how to maximize that value, and to help them determine what may have to be given up (or exchanged) for a particular deal.

Every deal is predicated on a story about the future. Therefore, strong deal preparation includes mastering the narrative about the outlook and tailoring it to your audience (e.g., lenders and equity investors). Few transactions generate their return from the historical or even current state, absent a direct play into assets (e.g., acquiring fixed assets at a discount to their market value). The return on investment is going to be driven by future performance.

Every deal is predicated on a story about the future. Therefore, strong deal preparation includes mastering the narrative about the outlook and tailoring it to your audience.

I have identified four areas critical to deal execution: (1) decipherability, (2) credibility, (3) growth story, and (4) acceleration. As with the finance spectrum, these four elements sequentially build on one another. It is valuable to incorporate these elements into the day-to-day management of a business. They are the foundation behind the maxim, "A business should always be ready to transact." We will discuss these elements individually and how the finance function plays a role in each.

DECIPHERABILITY

Anyone who assesses a transaction opportunity expects a clear and accurate view of the target company. Decipherability is the degree of insight into the financials, operational data, structural integrity, and standalone operations.

Decipherability is the first element for optimal deal execution, and it's all about data. No matter how successful and profitable a company may be, keeping good records that reconcile financial performance is critical for future deal execution. Therefore, business owners must understand how to create a clear, accurate view of their historical performance. It is difficult for anyone to analyze or manage a business if the right data is not being produced. Without available or accurate data, a business owner has no way to communicate what is working other than saying, "Trust me." Additionally, what do you think an owner or buyer will

No matter how successful and profitable a company may be, keeping good records that reconcile financial performance is critical for future deal execution.

conclude about projections from a company that cannot offer a clear view into the past? It should be easier to see into a mirror than a crystal ball!

In chapter 6 we discussed EBITDA and its common use as a reference metric for valuation. Without decipherability, you run the risk of not having a clear and defendable view of EBITDA. This will impact valuation negotiations and could potentially keep you from transacting altogether.

There are many reasons why a business could have poor decipherability. Perhaps the owner did not keep good books or simply did not have a system for tracking certain information. This may be understandable due to a lack of resources, but often we come across businesses that did not focus on capturing and organizing information because they thought it did not matter. That's a big mistake.

This happens frequently in family-run businesses where family (personal) expenses are being run through the company. They may have family on the payroll who do not play an active or full-time role in the business. The business might also own real estate that has little (or nothing) to do with the actual business operations. The fact that these exist inside a business is not necessarily a problem. The problem arises when those non-business items cannot be clearly separated when presenting the core business.

A common finance metric for valuation and deal discussions is "Adjusted EBITDA." Put simply, Adjusted EBITDA is the presentation of EBITDA that a buyer is purchasing, and may differ from the EBITDA in your financials. The number coming right off the financial statements is referred to as "Reported EBITDA," and if it is Reported EBITDA over the last twelve months, it is "LTM EBITDA." The difference between the two includes adjustments for changes to the business (e.g., you signed a new large customer to a long-term contract one month ago) and the strip-out of one-time, non-recurring, or extraordinary items that are not expected going forward. There is a long list of potential EBITDA adjustments, such as family or personal expenses, consultant costs, contract changes, discontinued operations, etc. If you are going to engage in any deal focused on EBITDA, be prepared to present the version of EBITDA that somebody will actually buy. This is critical for deal success, so we will dive deeper to show how this comes into play during transaction processes.

Quality of Earnings (QoE) Analysis

A buyer or investor may require a Quality of Earnings (QoE) analysis before completing a transaction. QoE is the most common third-party verification of EBITDA that is used in a sale process, especially those where the buyer is a private equity firm. The QoE provider scours the financial presentation of a business to identify differences between a company's accounting and generally accepted accounting principles (GAAP). Also, the QoE analysis will dig into the differences, if any, between Reported EBITDA and Adjusted EBITDA.

QoE strips away non-recurring activities that will not impact the financials going forward. If a business has non-business expenses, such as personal or family expenditures, QoE accounts for the fact that these will not exist under new ownership. Of course, completing this analysis is predicated on the ability of the owner to clearly distinguish non-business expenses in their data and records (i.e., decipherability). If the owner claims there are a number of these expenses but cannot provide evidence or documentation, the QoE provider is not going to give them the benefit of the doubt in their report.

QoE analysis often begins from LTM EBITDA as presented by the company. However, a lot can happen over twelve months. One of the goals of QoE is to understand how things have changed in order to present a baseline for annual financial performance as of the time of a transaction. This includes customer changes, product mix shifts, gross margin movements, changes in overhead expenses, etc.

QoE is an important component of due diligence given the role of EBITDA in valuation, and adjustments to EBITDA are a hot button topic. Here are a few simple examples of the adjustment analysis. Let us take a business with an LTM EBITDA of $10 million. The owner would like to sell the business, but before that happens all of the customers leave. Well, as of today and going forward, the Adjusted EBITDA is at best zero. On the flip side, let us say all the customers are happy and are staying around on long-term contracts. One of the large customers of the business is relatively new, and signed a contract three months ago that contributed $1 million to that LTM EBITDA. Here, if the company is sold, the owner deserves credit for the annual value of that customer contract. Adjusting for the full-year impact (as if that contract had been in place a full year) would add $3 million to LTM EBITDA, bringing our Adjusted EBITDA number to $13 million. Two scenarios, same LTM EBITDA, wildly different Adjusted EBITDA.

There are two other definitions of EBITDA you may come across, which are Run-Rate EBITDA and Pro-Forma EBITDA. Often synonymous with Adjusted EBITDA, these definitions are sometimes used to bridge historical performance with a view of the next twelve months (NTM, versus LTM). An example would be a growing subscription business that has a user base today that is much larger than a few months ago and has signed contracts to bring on more users in the near future. The company will want to position and present its financial performance to get credit for all users, even the ones who have not yet started but have signed contracts. Although we will not cover every nuance of these different definitions, I want you to be aware of them so you can be steely-eyed when a private equity buyer sits across the table from you talking about Pro-Forma NTM EBITDA. And with that, I promise I will not introduce any more definitions of EBITDA throughout the remainder of this book.

Depending on the complexity of a business, a QoE analysis can cost anywhere between $20,000 and $500,000. The larger and more complex the business, and the messier the data, the more you should expect it to cost. This cost is often incurred by the buyer or investor (although transaction expenses may get paid out of funds at closing), and as a result prospective buyers are going to be less excited about an opportunity if they expect difficult QoE and due diligence processes.

Therefore, the more work a business owner can do upfront, the better the business will look and the less the potential buyers or investors will have to do on their dime. Preparation is valuable and builds credibility by showing that the management team understands the importance of decipherability. This is true for purposes of a transaction *and* in managing the business day-to-day.

There is a trend developing within the SMB market where businesses with solid decipherability are getting a head start on transaction processes by completing a "QoE-lite." This may include in-house and third-party analysis equivalent to a QoE that the company presents to prospective buyers when marketing a deal. Often referred to as "sell-side QoE," it is a big credibility generator when dropped on the table in front of prospective buyers when they walk in the door. Completing sell-side QoE may not prevent a buyer from bringing in their own third party (they may want "their guy" whom they trust from an independence perspective), but the credibility remains. The previous work completed will also mean a buyer's QoE analysis will be faster and less costly. Especially in smaller businesses, we should not underestimate the impact of lower expected transaction costs for speed, negotiations, and even valuation.

Poor Decipherability Can Be a Show Stopper

One of the biggest challenges around decipherability is that it is hard to recreate over time. First Water recently sold a niche distribution business that was founded thirty years ago by a husband and wife. They'd built a fantastic business and had a well-respected brand name in their market. They were very profitable and did not have a complicated operation with one facility and twenty-five employees. They were able to keep their finger on the pulse because they were there every day, saw every order, processed every payment, cut every check, etc.

The owners engaged First Water because they were ready to sell the business and retire. In our discussion, I highlighted several areas for improvement that would make the process smoother, faster, and support them in getting the highest valuation possible for their company. They went home and realized they might not be ready to walk away. I told them to take all the time they needed, however, I advised that all the topics discussed would be important to consider if they *ever* wanted to sell the business.

Six months later, they asked me to lunch and were ready to go. They wanted to sell, but with one major caveat—they did not want to do any of things I recommended to prepare. While this was not ideal, I explained that we could still proceed. I told them there would be a number of ways that the deal process could be impacted, including who might be interested, the time it would take, valuation, and the transaction structure.

The biggest problem going into the potential deal was that the company had not been tracking their inventory. They had over five thousand products and no inventory management system. In their minds, they never thought they needed one because they were in the warehouse every day. They could walk up and down the aisles every day and see the stock levels. They did not see a need to invest capital into something that seemed unnecessary to their continued success.

From a finance perspective, this was a major problem. If a distribution company does not know its inventory (and therefore unit cost), then it really does not know its profitability either. And without an inventory balance, we could not calculate EBITDA. I expected this would be a problem and one that lacked a solution absent pausing the process for many months in order to put a system in place to generate information on product profitability (gross margins, in this case). Even if we did that, we could not re-create historical information without an enormous amount of brain damage. We did not have a time machine to go back three years and do a detailed reconciliation of the inventory!

We launched a sale process without any decipherability into this data. And even without verified inventory, buyers were interested. Let us not forget this was, and still is, a great business. We brought a bunch of people to the table, we negotiated, we received a number of letters of intent (LOIs), we picked a group, and we signed a deal! But the story did not end there.

Following the LOI, there typically comes an exclusivity period where the seller agrees they will only negotiate with that buyer long enough for the buyer to complete their formal due diligence on the business.

As expected, one of the first things the prospective buyer did was hire a firm for QoE. Unfortunately, the data was not there for them to complete the analysis in a timely and cost-effective way. Because of the lack of information, some smart people with smart processes had bad data. This is a rough spot, and the QoE provider had no choice but to make overly conservative assumptions. They did not want to be accused by the buyer of missing something, so in the absence of verifiable data, they did not give the benefit of the doubt. It is worth noting that the QoE provider is hired by the buyer, even though their role is as an independent third party.

The QoE provider formed a view on Adjusted EBITDA, and not surprisingly it was lower than our view. As a result, the prospective buyers were no longer comfortable doing the deal originally agreed to in the LOI. They wanted to renegotiate the deal. We were still comfortable in our own analysis of EBITDA, but the potential buyer was not willing to take the time and money to dig deeper. As a result, we had to either recut the deal or end the process with that buyer and go seek out one of the other alternatives.

In re-negotiating the deal, we had to add structure. One of the things that we did was negotiate an earn-out where the buyers would pay additional money to the sellers if financial performance was at or above certain thresholds in the following years. This was structured in a way such that if our view of EBITDA was correct, the sellers would receive an amount similar to the original deal, with some additional upside if the business performed well.

This required the sellers to realize a good chunk of the sale proceeds over time, instead of all upfront. This could be good or bad. It would be good if the business grew and the sellers earned even more than the original deal. It would be bad if performance declined or the business failed under the new ownership. These contingent amounts were at risk and dependent on the company's continued viability and success. The structure added some upside potential, but for sellers thinking about retirement the lack of decipherability left more at risk than they would have preferred.

The data shortcomings did not keep these owners from executing a transaction. All things considered, the valuation was solid. However, the deal structure added some risk to the realization of proceeds from the sale of their business. Money today is worth more than money tomorrow. Had the systems and data been in place, deal execution would have been better. This points to one of the primary benefits of having a Relational Finance specialist around the table: a Relational Finance specialist can assist with the preparation work irrespective of the timing of the transaction, while still playing the same advisory role in the deal process when the time is right.

This example is a poster child for how decipherability impacts a deal. For thirty years they did not need these internal capabilities to run a profitable, market-leading business. However, they absolutely needed them to optimize transaction execution.

I had an open and transparent dialogue with these owners. It was their choice not to make the incremental investments in the business solely for the purpose of maximizing sale proceeds. They understood they would likely leave money on the table, and they made their decision with full knowledge of the potential downsides. With that said, they could have avoided this dilemma had they made the investments throughout their ownership of the company. Do not wait until deal time! The earlier you start preparing, the better. Better yet, run the business as "always ready to transact." That is impossible without decipherability.

CREDIBILITY

Credibility is the next element for deal success. It is both a people- and process-driven element. Credibility centers around showing that the team is credible in managing the business and executing the business growth story. This solidifies the connection between better teams and better deals.

If decipherability is about data, credibility is about processes and controls which leverage that data. These processes include things like management functions, base financial processes (accounting, receivables, payables, etc.), budgeting, forecasting, scenario analysis, etc.

Credibility is established and enhanced through good information flow. The addition of documented processes makes the business more likely to withstand "people shocks" or "key man risk" by making it easier to transition responsibilities and integrate new team members. This is especially true in sale transactions where the CEO is the owner and is planning to leave the business (or at least leave the CEO seat).

We recently worked with a private equity firm that had acquired a family-owned manufacturing business. The business was run by a family for decades and the son had developed into the patriarch. He grew the business into an industry powerhouse by the time of the sale.

Every strategic decision in this business was made in a deer blind between the son and his right-hand man. Unfortunately, the family viewed finance as something that cost them money as opposed to saving or making them money. You may be surprised to find out that the business had several hundred million dollars of revenue and they did not have a single dedicated finance professional!

The son was a serial entrepreneur. He had built a heck of a business and was likely one of the best in the world at what he did. The problem for the son, like many entrepreneurs, was that eventually he wanted to walk away and seek out his next adventure. In his wake, there were severe limitations of data flow and forecast-ability. This made it difficult for the company to present a credible plan (the growth and capital roadmaps) to potential buyers.

Fortunately for them, they had an industry-specific Enterprise Resource Planning (ERP) system. As a result, they had a great deal of data, but they were not harnessing it. The private equity buyer observed they did not have sufficient line of sight into the business performance or outlook. Also, this lack of core projection capabilities hurt the credibility of the presented budget. All this for a buyer who requires significant growth in profits to reach the targeted return on investment.

These factors all became known to the private equity firm during their due diligence. They knew the son played a very important role in this business. They also knew there were no finance people inside the business. Because of these limitations, there were reservations about the growth outlook for the business, and about whether the remaining team in place would be the right group for the next phase under private equity ownership.

The private equity firm foresaw the work they would need to undertake upon acquiring this company. They knew they would have to spend time and capital building out the finance function. Without critical processes in place, they did not know what might "jump out of the weeds" and catch them by surprise. To help bridge the gap, we came in after the close of the deal to create better insight into company performance and to better harness the ERP data across the business.

So, this private equity firm knew what they were getting into. They had some blind spots, they knew they were going to incur additional costs, and they knew they were going to need to add or possibly replace members of senior management (including a new CEO). Do you think that impacted their valuation? You bet it did. It is a completely different dynamic when a buyer is highly confident that all the people and processes are in place when they buy the company.

When a business presents a projection as part of the transaction, a potential buyer analyzes that view with a critical, even doubtful, eye. Often, there will still be a fair number of unknowns that can impact the valuation and/or the transaction structure. With that in mind, part of the private equity firm's deal required the seller (i.e., the outgoing CEO/business owner) to rollover a chunk of his ownership into the new deal so that he would be incentivized to stay engaged and be helpful to the new owners. Millions and millions of dollars, the potential to either make or lose them, tends to be a hyper-driver of human behavior!

If there had been more credibility in the team and in the processes, the seller would have realized better deal execution. The buyers certainly would have felt more confident, and buyers who feel more confident pay more money. The buyer may have also been in a better position to act on strategic initiatives (execute on the growth story) and get out in front of certain market trends that presented risks for the business and industry. Instead, a significant amount of time and capital was utilized in creating core processes after the deal.

In this example, the seller made out fine, in the way that selling your company for a couple hundred million dollars seems fine. However, this is not always the case, and nobody really knows what was left on the table here. A business owner needs to be able to show credibility around the team leading the business and the core processes used in managing the business. Not only does credibility matter for the story being told for the deal, but it also relevant for the team's ability to execute on that story following a transaction. People and processes go hand in hand. A business has to

People and processes go hand in hand. A business has to have both.

have both. A business owner cannot have a bad team and a good story, or a good team and a bad story. There should be no weak links.

The credibility of management in pitching the growth story can be the difference maker in a deal. Just because a CEO has never run a larger company before does not make having that CEO at the helm a "deal killer." However, to be convincing, the team has to prove it is capable or that others will be brought in with the requisite experience.

We see successful entrepreneurs and founders step aside and bring in a CEO more than you may realize. This tends to happen for one of two reasons: (1) a business owner is sufficiently self-aware and business-aware of what the company needs to flourish and realizes he or she does not have the proper skill set, or (2) the decision gets forced upon the owner because of hiccups in business performance.

A business owner (or CEO) needs to be able to reflect and honestly answer, "Can I adapt and evolve to meet the growing needs of this company?" If the answer is yes, then great. But if not, that is okay as well. If the expertise of the owner is in product development and now time is consumed with managing a rapidly growing company, maybe it makes sense to step aside and focus on that core competency. Businesses need widget masters, data masters, business masters, capital masters, etc. We talk about the growth and capital roadmaps, but there is an important people roadmap as well that contributes to both.

GROWTH STORY

If the best part of finance is storytelling, then the importance of this element cannot be overstated. Successful deals are characterized by the

> ***Successful deals are characterized by the mastery of storytelling.***

mastery of storytelling. Therefore, the ability of a business owner to be a persuasive storyteller can help get the best terms on a deal. Here we are in the chapter on better deals, talking about growth. This is not a coincidence.

On a simplistic level, the number one question a growth story should answer is, "Where is the growth coming from?" The questions are going to be asked, so the key is proactively telling a story backed by data and a detailed plan. Will the business sell more of its products in existing markets? Or will it be via geographic expansion? Maybe it is launching complementary products and services? Acquiring other companies that enhance existing product offerings? Whatever the pitch, the storyteller also needs to lay out the amount of capital needed and prospective risks associated with the growth plan.

Some of the biggest companies in the world right now have never made a dollar in profits (e.g., Uber, Tesla, etc.) and yet in both public and private markets they can have valuations in the tens of billions of dollars (at least at the time of writing this book). You may ask, "How can this be?" It is because the leaders of those businesses are tremendous storytellers. They can connect the work they are doing with a different looking future. As a result, they are able to raise substantial amounts of capital. Often, they are so good at it that they do not even need a great capital roadmap since they can tap capital at will. They are able to raise capital solely on the strength of their communication of the growth and market opportunity, and they can convince the market that their teams are the ones who will be able to realize that vision. They can engage employees, engage customers, and ultimately engage capital. And it all happens through telling stories.

Linking a growth story to a financial outcome is vital in almost every deal. This step is part of the alignment of the growth and capital roadmaps. In many ways, the growth story and the growth roadmap are synonymous. The biggest difference is the tailoring of the roadmap to a specific audience—you can tell different stories with the same roadmap!

A potential buyer or investor will want to understand the financial requirements and outcome of realizing the growth roadmap/story. How much capital will it take to get there? If we succeed, what does that look like for our investment? Therefore, business owners should not underestimate how important it is to have a capital roadmap that supports the growth story. Credibility requires knowledge of both and how they are interconnected. In fact, the interplay of the growth and capital roadmaps is a core capability within the planning component of the finance spectrum. It shows that the business owner has thought about it, understands how to finance it, and knows the steps it will take to get there. Combined, all of these components equate to a much more believable story.

If the purpose of data is dialogue, then a business owner cannot underestimate how critical it is to tailor the growth story to the audience. Without speaking directly to the perspectives on the other side of the table, it does not matter how good your roadmaps are. Tailoring the same growth story for multiple audiences is an invaluable skill that strong leaders develop over time. To create a compelling growth story, a business owner must be able to communicate (1) where the growth will come from, (2) what the market outlook and timeline for accomplishing the growth is, (3) the capital roadmap attached to the growth story, and (4) how the growth and capital roadmaps fit the target risk-return profile of the counterparty.

The appropriate capital roadmap for the growth roadmap is a critical item to determine upfront since it ensures the right people are in the room. A business owner should not pitch a capital need without ensuring it is a good fit for the risk and return profile of the capital provider sitting across the table (not to mention the investment size, structure, timeline, etc.). This should be determined before the conversation starts.

Pitching a bank for a loan as compared to pitching an investor for growth equity capital are very different beasts, and high-growth businesses will likely be doing both simultaneously. For example, a growth equity investor might expect a 30 percent compounded return on invested capital. If a business owner tells a growth and capital story that offers a 5 percent return, it is not very interesting. Therefore, business owners need to be able to communicate the story in the context of the perspective of each investor, including the investment amount, risk, and return profile.

Unless a business owner plans on selling and walking away immediately, the actual realization point of most deals is somewhere off into the future. Because so many transactions are predicated on a future outlook (that is often a bigger and/or more profitable company than the current state), credibility around the growth roadmap is paramount. That growth is key to the success of the deal, for one or both parties.

In order to tell the right growth story, there are several other components to consider to be convincing, including:

Sector/Market Outlook

If a business owner believes the company is going to naturally grow 25 percent a year in an industry that grows 3 percent a year, then a buyer or investor will want to clearly understand how growth will outpace the overall industry. Consider a business owner growing 25 percent a year in an industry that may be declining or is subject to disruption—like we are seeing today with brick and mortar retail stores. We are living in the age of online retailers like Amazon. It is impossible to think about brick and mortar retail concepts without addressing how e-commerce impacts that market. Therefore, failure to incorporate these dynamics into a growth story would certainly harm the credibility of the team.

I currently live in Houston, which is a major hub for energy companies. The price of oil seems to run in cycles and can be volatile. If the outlook for a sector is poor, then there is a high likelihood that this will impact the timeline associated with the growth story. Insight into cyclicality and other macro factors is fundamental for a good growth story, including the timeline. Operating at the peak or on the downside of a cycle may make it more difficult to realize aggressive timelines.

Key Man Risk

Smart buyers account for the fact that owners typically know the most about their business. The owner is often the most important person (i.e., the "key man") to the success of the business, or even its ability to operate altogether. This is precisely why sales often involve a rollover of equity or an earn out component. A larger business of over $100 million in revenue is more likely to have a bigger team with more capabilities and embedded processes than a business a tenth of that size. Bigger teams equate to more knowledge and responsibility outside of the business owner, and hopefully sales and operational processes that can flourish in the absence of the owner. If 50 or 100 percent of the knowledge walks out the door the day a transaction closes, this can be a major challenge for deal negotiations. If the objective of an owner is to walk away as part of the deal, he or she must ensure the team can execute the proposed growth story, key man or not.

Personal Objectives

Every deal should dovetail with the personal objectives of the owner. This includes transaction structure, partner selection, and how both impact short- and long-term goals. Those goals need to first be identified. From there, growth, capital, and deal variables should work with those objectives, or at the very least, around them.

Consider next a business owner with significant growth opportunities who has a desire to pass the business down to the next generation. The opportunity implies that the company would grow faster than it can fund internally (i.e., by reinvesting profits). Millions of dollars are needed to build a new facility, which is far beyond current annual profits. It would take years to save up the capital for the new facility, and the growth opportunity is now.

Let us assume the growth opportunity is too fast and risky for a bank or any lender to fund, so to take full advantage of the opportunity the business would need to bring in an equity partner. The growth and capital roadmaps are identified, but there is a problem: the personal objective of passing the business on means retaining 100 percent ownership of the business. Because of this, the growth and capital roadmaps are actually misaligned, simply because personal preferences impact what the owner is willing to accept. Only one of two things can happen here. Either the growth roadmap has to change, or the personal preference has to shift to allow for some equity dilution to achieve the faster growth.

Incorporating personal preferences into the growth and capital roadmaps is essential to roadmap design. Business owners should never enter into a deal that runs counter to what they are trying to accomplish personally. This may seem like common sense, but this happens all the time and it usually happens because of a "blind spot." Business owners sometimes unintentionally restrict themselves by having a "whatever it takes" attitude to bring an immediate opportunity to fruition, even if it runs counter to their long-term plans or goals.

Track Record of Growth

Another component of a good growth story is management's demonstration of a growth-oriented mentality. Often, the leaders and owners of SMBs have never run a larger company before. Through the act of growing to where they are now, they have demonstrated their ability to run a larger and larger company. For example, a business owner running a $30 million revenue business, which was grown from $10 million, may have never run a $30 million business before. But when it was a $10 million business, that was also a first. Showing the evolution of the management of the business from one stage to the next is a surefire way to build credibility that you have what it takes to take on the next rung of the ladder.

Growth is difficult, risky, and takes time and capital. Business owners do not always want to maximize their growth potential because they do not want the added risk or they do not want to bring in outside capital. These owners might be happy chugging along right where they are. However, if they ever want to do a deal, it is critically important that they still understand how to construct an attractive growth story, since the capital partner may be more willing to take the risks and invest the capital to hit the gas pedal.

When First Water begins working on a new deal with a partner company, the first thing I ask them to do is write the press release. I strongly believe that if a business owner cannot synthesize the "why" for a deal in a few sentences (*including* why their counterparty would be excited about the transaction), we need to go back to the drawing board. I find this to be a great sanity check before launching a formal deal process.

Finance is the vein that connects teams with data and companies with capital. Connecting teams with data has everything to do with having the right information to analyze, manage, project, and grow your business. Connecting companies with capital is about telling the right story that is backed by management credibility and an outlook supported by data and related finance capabilities. A Relational Finance specialist is the only one who can help with *all* of these pieces. Unlike traditional finance models, steps can also be taken well in advance of a transaction process.

Connecting companies with capital is about telling the right story that is backed by management credibility and an outlook supported by data and related finance capabilities.

Make Working Capital Work for You

Growth is expensive—hiring people, investing in additional production capacity, buying more materials, all while customers pay you in thirty days, sixty days, or longer. As is typical when growing, the business needs more working capital in order to fund operations and to deliver products and services. Bless all the businesses that get deposits or prepayments from their customers!

Funding working capital is a critical component of the growth and capital roadmaps. I consider it part of the capital roadmap since it is often funded through debt financing, such as a line of credit or receivables/inventory line with a bank. This type of funding tends to have the cheapest cost of capital, with equity capital on the other end of the spectrum because it is dilutive to ownership. Setting yourself up to access working capital funding allows you to minimize the cash you must keep in the business while managing the ups and downs. Buyers focus on this to determine how much of their own capital they need to use to purchase a company and fund future operations. Generally speaking, they do not want to use any more than they have to.

We see many businesses that elect to keep extra cash in the business because they are debt-adverse, want to reduce liquidity risk, and/or know they have limitations in their ability to project their future needs. We do not fault the business or the owners for this, unless of course they want to do a deal. In many situations where First Water has advised, the company has not done the prep work in order to put this kind of funding in place. During deal processes, this becomes apparent to an investor or buyer, and if they believe they need to keep more cash in the business because of the historical practice, it is going to cost you. Whether in valuation or a mechanism called a "working capital adjustment," not doing the work on working capital can hurt a seller.

Cash that is tied up is capital that has a cost. Financial buyers like private equity are hyper-focused on maximizing the return on the capital they deploy, so make sure you show them how much they will need to fund your business operations and growth story. Not surprisingly, the capabilities around figuring this out are right there in the finance function with data, reporting, projections, planning, and capital. The earlier you focus on those capabilities prior to engaging in a deal process, the better.

Mergers and Acquisitions (M&A)

Before we leave our discussion on growth stories, I want to break out the topic of mergers and acquisitions (M&A). Mergers and acquisitions are an attractive component of the growth story to financial investors like private equity, as they specifically like opportunities where they can use the balance sheet (debt and/or equity, including their capital) to increase the size of their companies. In the private equity world, a business that can support additional M&A is called a "platform." It is called a platform because other companies can be "bolted on" to it, and the acquisitions themselves are called "add-ons." A platform that completes a number of add-ons within its same space (e.g., buying regional competitors to create a national company) is called a "roll-up." Financial buyers *love* roll-ups.

Therefore, the potential for future M&A should be considered in the development of the growth story. From a valuation perspective, M&A potential can also increase the EBITDA multiple that gets applied to a business today, because the buyer can see the accretive benefits of acquisitions. These benefits manifest in two ways. The first and more obvious is cost savings and synergies. When two companies are combined, there is usually an opportunity to reduce overhead (e.g., combining two offices into one), to streamline operations (e.g., two competitors operating at 70 percent capacity should be able to create one company operating closer to 100 percent), and to realize other economies of scale (e.g., getting volume discounts by ordering more from vendors).

Here is an example. Two companies, both with $5 million EBITDA and both worth a multiple of five times EBITDA ($25 million each), decide to combine in a fifty-fifty merger. As part of that merger, they were able to realize $2 million worth of cost savings, all of which drops through to EBITDA. By combining, they created not a $10 million EBITDA company, but a $12 million EBITDA company. At that same multiple of five, the combined company is now worth $60 million, where the two separate companies were worth $25 million each, or $50 million total. They created $10 million of value through cost savings and synergies.

Second, M&A provides the opportunity for something called "multiple arbitrage." This is one of the great tools of private equity. The core of the arbitrage is this: larger companies trade for higher EBITDA multiples. This has to do with the perceived stability of larger businesses, the options by which those companies can be financed, the type of capital that is available to invest in those opportunities (e.g. larger investment funds), and the competition for M&A among larger players.

Here is how it works. Take that company with $5 million of EBITDA worth five times EBITDA ($25 million). It has the opportunity to acquire a smaller competitor with $2 million EBITDA. Because of the smaller size, let us assume the valuation multiple on the smaller company is three ($6 million value). So, our acquirer pays $6 million, and now has a company with $7 million of EBITDA (let's ignore cost savings). Now the combined company is worth $35 million (seven multiplied by five) and, with the $6 million acquisition, we increased total value by $10 million, creating a $4 million arbitrage.

Now, we repeat this two more times: acquiring $4 million more of EBITDA for $12 million (two companies of $2 million EBITDA at a multiple of three each). Now we have an $11 million EBITDA company built through $18 million of M&A (three acquisitions at $6 million each). Here is the kicker: because our platform is now bigger, let us say its multiple has increased from five to six. Our $11 million of EBITDA is now worth $66 million. We started at $25 million worth of value, completed $18 million of M&A, and ended up with $66 million total value. We have created $23 million ($66 – $18 – $25) of arbitrage. Needless to say, this is good math!

Understanding how future M&A could play a role in your business is critical, even if you never plan to do it yourself. A business owner who starts thinking about this, identifying potential M&A targets, and even engaging with some of these groups will have a better growth story to tell as part of a transaction. Remember, part of telling the most impressive growth story is tailoring it to your audience.

ACCELERATION

If a business owner's growth story is the telling of the growth roadmap, then acceleration is the progress along that roadmap. Acceleration is a "nice to have" element of deal making. Not having it at the time of a deal will not kill you, but it sure does not hurt.

If a business owner plans to sell his or her company, acceleration overlaps with some of the buyer's work in due diligence. For example, a business owner may identify new potential customers and provide updates on the status of each of the prospects. Do this well and you'll get credit for it come valuation time through those additional sales, profits, pipeline, backlog, etc.

It is a similar opportunity on the expense side. If a business owner takes the time to identify operational improvements that will increase margins, a growth story that includes margin improvement (higher profitability) becomes much easier to tell. Take it one step further, from identification to implementation, and the improvements start showing up in the financials before the transaction. This is what acceleration is all about.

In discussing valuation, we have talked extensively about EBITDA, both how much you have and the multiple that will be applied to it. Acceleration is one of those elements that can impact both. Increasing EBITDA heading into a transaction provides a nice tailwind for successful deal execution.

We recently began working with a business that has been around for over twenty years. The company is a leader in the training and certification space. Historically the product was sold through print, but in the last couple of years they have tapped into new online video platforms. This has allowed them to reach a much larger audience worldwide in a scalable, high-margin fashion. While still in the early stages of realizing the full potential of this new channel, this has completely changed the financial and growth profile of the business. The owners are nearing retirement and ready to work on a sale process, but they have also been aggressively generating new content while partnering with additional video distribution partners.

This example is relevant because not only are the owners proving out their growth story, but they are also accelerating into a prospective deal via continued growth *and* building out a pipeline. Acceleration is a big endorsement of a team's credibility, and what is more powerful in communicating your growth story than by actively demonstrating that story is in motion?

Note that a growth story which is materially different from the historical path of the business is more challenging if action has not yet been taken to prove out the new trajectory. This is compounded if an owner is looking to sell and simultaneously walk away with no strings attached. A business owner must be prepared for questions like, "Why haven't you already accomplished this growth story if you have been at this for years?" or, "If you have all this upside growth potential, why are you looking to cash out now?"

Of course, there are plenty of reasonable and truthful ways a business owner might answer these questions. They might say, "I wasn't comfortable taking the risk," or "I didn't have the capital."

However, a business owner must still realize there may be a credibility challenge if pitching a future that looks far rosier than any other results the business had in the past.

If faced with a growth story that looks different than the historical performance of the business, acceleration is an immensely valuable way to show credibility around the new story being told. Not to mention it can help increase that EBITDA multiple if that new story has a more attractive growth profile than the legacy business.

When telling a growth story, put yourself in the seat of the person on the other side of the table. A debt provider will think differently than an equity partner, joint venture partner, merger partner, or private equity buyer. Different types of capital partners analyze a business and the growth story in different ways. The ability to speak directly to the other side in their terms results in better deals.

This is where a Relational Finance specialist can wield the diversity of perspective to help a business prepare for and execute on a deal process. Often in the role of translator, a Relational Finance specialist with experience working in private equity, lending, and investment banking can be an enormous asset on your side of the table. The best person for your side is someone who has sat in all the other seats!

DEAL EXECUTION

There are many moving parts involved in deal preparation and the communication of the growth story to make your deal an attractive target. And the journey does not end here. We still need to consider the steps and mechanics of negotiating and closing a deal.

This is not a textbook on the types of terms a business owner may see in different types of deals. Therefore, we are not going to delve into the nuances or typical contractual terms associated with different types of transactions. Covering the universe of different capital types, transaction structures, and the typical terms of those deals would turn this book into an anthology!

Instead, remember this: when considering a specific transaction, an owner should seek out resources to understand the type and variety of terms to anticipate. Do your research, and then find people you can trust who can advise you through each step of the process. Importantly, make sure those advisors are aligned with your goals!

When considering a specific transaction, an owner should seek out resources to understand the type and variety of terms to anticipate.

There are two points to discuss regarding the finance function's support of deal execution. The first one is simple; it is the negotiation of terms. If a business owner does not like a proposed deal offer, how should that be communicated and argued? The answer is: with data! Show the other side why the term is overly punitive or restrictive. The preference for certain deal terms often has to do with the perception of risk. Address that risk credibly, and you have the foundation for a good argument. That is certainly much better than saying, "I don't like that."

The second point to discuss is how the finance function helps business owners achieve more confidence that they are doing a good deal. This specifically relates to the projection and planning components of the finance spectrum. If a business owner does not have detailed growth and capital roadmaps, then trying to do a deal to raise capital will be difficult, if not impossible. If the capital can be raised, how will he or she know if it is enough? Or perhaps, maybe too much capital is raised. Without sounding like Goldilocks, too much and too little is suboptimal. We want just right. Leverage your finance function to thread the needle.

If insufficient capital is raised, the business owner will have to go back to the well and investors are not going to be happy because it was not the outlook they were pitched. Chances are it will be a difficult conversation, and the need for that conversation itself is often a credibility killer. You can bet that additional capital will be expensive. On the contrary, bringing in too much capital means more was given up (e.g., equity) than necessary. I like to know how hot my porridge is before I eat!

To avoid being in either of these situations, a business owner must put in the work upfront with projections and planning. This provides a better chance of structuring the right deal that fits the growth and capital roadmaps *and* gives up as little as possible.

Nothing is worse than making a deal that goes sideways right afterward. An example of this would be getting a loan that is out of compliance two months later. If a business owner does not have the ability to build out the future view (i.e., projections for growth and capital requirements), the business may end up in a real jam. With debt, this could mean default, foreclosure, or potentially losing the entire business because forward visibility was not properly incorporated into the deal structuring.

Even if getting it wrong does not kill a business, it will absolutely restrict its flexibility. The bank may not knock down the door (immediately) to repossess assets and collateral to repay a loan, but it certainly will not extend any more credit. A bad deal can significantly delay growth and other progress toward goals, and time is typically not a luxury for entrepreneurs.

The Right Deal

The right deal is the one aligned with a business owner's growth and capital roadmaps. The ability of an owner to cut the right deal may be the most critical step in the execution of those roadmaps.

Again, there is no one-size-fits-all when talking about the *right* deal. What's right for one business may not be right for another. That said, we have identified the three parts required for every right deal: (1) the growth roadmap, (2) the capital roadmap, and (3) stakeholder objectives. Let us conclude this chapter with a hypothetical example that illustrates all these components.

An owner in business for five years is ready to pull some money out so he can move his family out of an apartment and into a house. If he goes with a traditional bank loan to fund further business growth, he will likely be restricted from distributing profits out of his business (diverted to pay down the loan). If he does not realize this in advance, and then does the deal, he would unintentionally delay or lose his ability to accomplish other goals that were important to him. Getting this alignment right for smaller businesses is critical because the growth and capital roadmaps of the business intimately impact the growth and capital roadmaps of the owner's family!

The term "eyes wide open" also means extending vision to beyond the business to those personal preferences and making sure transaction options address both. Certain considerations, like willingness or risk tolerance, fall solely to the business owner.

We see too many business owners focus solely on deal terms like dollars, interest rates, price per share, and other quantitative factors. There are many more factors to consider, such as governance requirements, financial restrictions, or ownership dilution. All of it is part of the deal. A Relational Finance specialist brings awareness to all these factors, but especially the ones SMBs may overlook. When the growth and capital roadmaps are properly constructed, nothing gets glossed over.

By helping businesses take the time to design, align, and execute on these growth and capital roadmaps, the Relational Finance model is a valuable sidekick through all phases of a business owner's journey. This is enhanced by engagement flexibility and the ability to build a relationship without being purely transaction-oriented on the front end. In fact, transaction answers may not even be on the radar when we first get to work. The major benefit to this is that we can proactively plan, prepare, and be ready to strike when opportunity knocks. By running your company as well as possible, you also keep your eyes open and resources ready to process those opportunities. More knocks, more doors opened, more deals, more value created and monetized. Feels good to write it, but it's a lot more fun to do it!

CHAPTER 10

UNLEASH YOUR FINANCE FUNCTION!

Working with SMB owners is both rewarding and highly personal. Experiencing the rise of a business is also observing the rise of a family's future and legacy. We partner with people who trust us to carry them through major inflection points in their business, some of which the owner will go through only once in a lifetime. Now *that* is an opportunity to make an impact. It requires trust, and nothing embodies that level of trust more than an entrepreneur inviting you to the kids' birthday parties. We all understand the reason for working.

It is a real privilege to be able to assist business owners through phases in their businesses that are complicated and/or represent uncharted territory. Whether business owners need help inside their business, positioning for their retirement, or securing their family's financial wellbeing, Relational Finance is a path to holistic finance expertise that was previously only available piecemeal or simply unavailable to smaller businesses.

The world of finance remains heavily focused on transactional interactions. Relational Finance flips the status quo on its head by showing that there is still the ability to use finance as a mechanism to build relationships. With the structure of the traditional finance models underserving SMBs for far too long, working with SMBs is also a huge market opportunity.

Relational Finance flips the status quo on its head by showing that there is still the ability to use finance as a mechanism to build relationships.

In chapter 4, we discussed how traditional model restrictions boil down to two factors. First, it is a function of cost. The best talent and expertise has been traditionally outside the affordability of SMBs. And second, it is a function of access with SMBs previously unable to leverage valuable finance expertise unless they are ready to transact and do it right now.

We have a very particular set of skills that offers the opportunity to make a disproportionate impact in SMBs as compared to other advisors and models. Additionally, we are always getting better, learning from our partner companies as they learn from us. Continuous exposure to a variety of perspectives is what makes our work exciting. We are frequently able to draw parallels between businesses and industries based on our previous experiences. As a result, we are continuously improving, becoming better advisors, investors, and partners to the SMBs who partner with us.

I wrote this book for two different groups. First, for business owners and leaders. When the success or the profitability of a business means that a family eats, there is nothing more important. We help

SMBs whether they are looking to chase growth and maximize transaction execution (i.e., value monetization) or are looking to protect what they've built.

The goal of this book is to unearth the value of the finance function, discuss the traditional finance models, and show that SMBs have a new and improved option in Relational Finance. The finance function, and the way it is harnessed in managing a business, is not something taught in schools.

We are on a quest to change the way SMB owners think about finance, by redefining finance altogether in connecting teams with data and companies with capital. To accomplish this, we combine the tools, processes, people, and capital that amplify and protect the entrepreneurial spirit at the heart of all great companies. Through Relational Finance, we provide an accessible and aligned way for SMBs to access the full finance spectrum to start realizing the value of the finance function today.

Achieving better teams, better growth, and better deals is a goal for every business owner. Managing a business for more visibility and less risk means fewer surprises and a better night's sleep. It is hard to put a price or value on that, but we know it is high.

The second group of people I wrote this book for is other finance professionals. If sharing the secrets and success around Relational Finance causes them to explore this alternative model, then that is an additional benefit to the market and to businesses. I welcome professionals starting out in finance to pick up this book and consider alternatives to the traditional finance track, just like I did.

Traditional finance models do not have a glowing reputation in the business community. They have contributed to the whole Wall Street/Main Street dichotomy. This book shows how finance goes beyond transactional interactions. Finance is about insight, planning, setting and achieving goals, telling stories, and realizing the value that you have created. When harnessed, finance becomes a powerful tool in the toolbox of every business owner.

Finance is about insight, planning, setting and achieving goals, telling stories, and realizing the value that you have created. When harnessed, finance becomes a powerful tool in the toolbox of every business owner.

THE FUTURE OF FINANCE

Most of the owners and leaders of SMBs do not come from a finance background. We are pulling back the veil to expose the value of the finance function and empower SMBs with access. Leaders of growth-oriented companies know that reaching their goals requires different skills than what got them to where they are today. Finance is one of those skills.

Harnessing the power of the finance function can be a major differentiator for a business among its competitors. Not many people think about finance capabilities as providing a competitive edge, but they can be the catalyst to winning a market by acting faster, pricing better, making higher margins, allocating capital efficiently, and closing better deals on better terms.

Ten to fifteen years from the publishing of this book, much of what we have discussed here will be standard practice. With technological advances driving improvements in data, automation, and predictive capabilities, we are only scratching the surface. Navigating new options and selecting the right tools are skills in and of themselves. An abundance of options is not always a positive! The onus is on leaders to define their needs and invest in the tools that will align and accelerate their growth and capital roadmaps.

DEVELOPING A POWERFUL STORYLINE

The best part of finance is storytelling, and telling your story through the lens of finance is the only way to attract the capital to achieve your growth and monetization objectives. When done properly, business owners can address multiple capital audiences with confidence and pave a path to accomplishing their vision and monetizing their success.

> ***Telling your story through the lens of finance is the only way to attract the capital to achieve your growth and monetization objectives.***

At First Water, we leverage data, processes, and diverse finance perspectives to promote and support the human components of finance, including a culture of accountability, goal setting, and storytelling. The purpose of data is dialogue. Businesses are run by teams. There is no great story without a good ending, and thus I challenge you to keep the end in mind as you craft your own narrative.

When we identify what success looks like—the destination of our growth and capital roadmaps—we know that a confident decision is one that takes the next step along those paths. How do you climb a mountain? One step at a time! When today's decisions are linked to the end of the path, the result is higher confidence, lower stress, and a long-term mentality with your eyes keenly trained on the prize. All of these will accelerate your progress.

THE STAKES ARE HIGH

It is no surprise that financial missteps and lack of capital are big reasons why companies fail. Without the finance function, businesses get caught by surprise and/or run out of funding to realize their vision. There will always be "snakes in the grass," in that we cannot project everything (i.e., eliminate risk), but by prioritizing the finance function we ensure the lawn is mowed. By acting proactively in the face of an approaching reptile and having a game plan if one evades our sight, we won't worry about being caught off guard and will sleep better at night.

A business that does not have the best products or service can still beat its competitors with better talent, better sales, and better execution. Yet you do not typically see CEOs on television speaking to higher efficiency and reduced risk as their business plan. These things might not be as sexy as the product, but achieving better growth and better deals through avenues other than product quality can definitely be the difference between winning and losing.

THE TIME IS NOW

Historically, finance and the finance function only tend to come up in a business when something negative happens. That is changing as businesses recognize their value and have better options, such as Relational Finance. Businesses will invest in finance earlier than before, changing their priorities in team construction and leveraging outside expertise to build out the capabilities of the finance spectrum. This promotes engaged, aligned, and accountable teams with the information flow they need to all row in the same direction and change course when needed.

Great entrepreneurs have an uncanny intuition for their end markets and business operations. Their fingers are on the pulse, but they only have ten fingers. Inevitably, their success is the result of understanding which pulse is worthy of their focus. The time to delegate is before you run out of fingers! The best way to get big is to act big, and by investing in finance capabilities earlier, businesses can reach their goals faster and safer.

The best way to get big is to act big, and by investing in finance capabilities earlier, businesses can reach their goals faster and safer.

The finance function does not detract from the powerful entrepreneurial spirit that inspires and helps build successful companies. In fact, finance validates it, amplifies it, and accelerates it. The value of proactivity cannot be overstated, and managing reactively is like getting in a sports car with an empty gas tank. It might take longer to get where you want to go.

Speaking of getting where you want to go, a map and a weather forecast sure come in handy. Finance capabilities enable better performance visibility, projectability, and scenario analysis, giving business owners the ability to take control of their outlook. With the right data and forecasting tools, you can accelerate along your roadmap while simultaneously attracting the capital (gasoline!) to propel you to your destination.

Success or failure is often a function of time. While a detour may not be the equivalent of driving into a ditch, the scenic route means you may get beaten to the finish line. An investment in preparation is an investment in speed, and avoiding bad deals keeps you on the fastest route. I've made my points with the car analogy, so I will tie a bow on it by saying finance can be the difference between a Ferrari and a jalopy.

A KEY FOR ROADMAP SUCCESS

Plenty of owners have successful businesses in spite of little or no finance capabilities. While this is a testament to exactly how powerful the entrepreneurial spirit is, it is not the way to achieve better teams, better growth, or better deals. This is especially true if the end goal is to sell. As shared through numerous examples, the absence of the finance function and related capabilities will negatively impact transaction execution. Finance may not be the most important corporate function for business success, but if a business owner wants to achieve long-term growth and value maximization, it is certainly a critical component.

Business success is not defined by historical results or by this year's income. Instead, success is the ability to maximize value over time through the alignment and execution of the growth and capital roadmaps. A relentless commitment to the roadmaps also ensures that a business owner will be ready to transact when the time is right.

Along those roadmaps, there are numerous inflection points where Relational Finance is particularly valuable. These inflection points might be characterized by the business owner seeking to accomplish one or more of the following:

- expanding significantly with the recognition that the team needs incremental skills and capabilities to take control of the growth and successfully manage a larger enterprise;
- acquiring incremental capital funding to accomplish growth and/or internal investment objectives;

- completing a transaction, or transactions, in the near or intermediate future, which may include taking chips off the table (i.e., monetizing some or all of ownership); and
- acquiring complementary companies as a means of growth, diversification, and/or scale.

Take notice that these catalysts are framed around the business owner's goals, which is where the conversations start.

RELATIONAL FINANCE IS THE WAY

Many aspects of professional service models are "black boxes," creating engagement rigidity to allow the service businesses to scale more easily. This is a reason why SMBs have lacked access to finance expertise. The finance experts are sitting inside business models whose engagement catalysts may not align with the needs of SMBs.

Relational Finance offers a customized, cost effective, and aligned approach with the flexibility to tailor relationships to business and owner objectives and goals. This makes Relational Finance a fit for a wide range of businesses and circumstances, which is by design. However, its greatest purpose is to go deeper into individual relationships over a longer period of time. This offers the best opportunity to make a meaningful impact on a business owner's journey, contribute to value creation, and participate in monetization. This is undeniably a win-win on multiple levels.

There are both quantitative and qualitative benefits to having better teams, better growth, and better deals. The quantitative side is simple: efficiency, growth, value, monetization. However, the qualitative side is at the core of more of our conversations with business owners. Those include: reducing surprises, feeling more confident about decision-making, and ultimately sleeping better at night. These benefits are hard to measure. You cannot open the *Wall Street Journal* and find today's price for peace of mind.

You cannot open the* Wall Street Journal *and find today's price for peace of mind.

My personal mission is to make the business owner's journey more efficient and enjoyable, helping to realize envisioned growth while maximizing and ultimately monetizing value. As Relational Finance spreads, more SMBs will embrace the finance function and related capabilities. Do you want to be on the front end or the back end of this movement? Staying in neutral too long when everyone else around you is accelerating means neutral is the same as going in reverse. And no one *wants* to be in reverse.

THE FINANCE READINESS (FIRE) SCORE

What's the next step?

The Finance Readiness Score or "FiRe Score" is an assessment tool created by First Water to advance the discussion about how finance capabilities help business owners achieve their goals faster and with less risk, all with an eye toward maximizing value creation and deal execution. Your FiRe Score highlights whether your finance capabilities are aligned with your growth/transaction objectives and the risks of managing your business.

Leveraging our experience in working with a myriad of different businesses (and talking to countless others), we have developed target "readiness" ranges based on the level of your aspirations and implied risk. This valuable tool was built with questions that seek to reveal the level of aggressiveness around growth and transaction objectives, the level of risk embedded within your business, and the state of your current finance processes and capabilities.

Combined, the answers provided to these questions create an overall finance, growth, and deal readiness rating. No matter how good (or not so good) the FiRe Score may reveal your readiness to be, we pose additional questions for you to focus on your growth and capital roadmaps. Of course, no simple assessment can capture every nuance of your unique business, but FiRe Score is the next step in igniting the dialogue.

> ***Determine your FiRe Score at www.fire-score.com and use it to take stock on how finance capabilities (data, reporting, forecasting, planning, and capital) can impact your business. The finance function can transform your business, and with Relational Finance you can unleash the power of better teams, better growth, and better deals.***

CLOSING THOUGHTS

Relational Finance is the ideal finance model for SMBs. It was created and iterated specifically for the needs of SMB owners based on the shortcomings of traditional models. However, it is not an indictment of those traditional models, which continue to offer valuable expertise and capital into the marketplace. Relational Finance enables cost-effective access to finance capabilities without the inherent conflicts embedded in transactional models, and one of the many benefits of Relational Finance is being able to better utilize the traditional models with a partner on your side of the table with "other side" experience.

When I started First Water in 2010, I knew a problem existed, but I did not know the answer. If I could crack the code of the SMB finance gap, I knew the impact would be explosive. Like many entrepreneurs with whom we have partnered, I jumped off a cliff not knowing how I was going to construct that parachute. What I did not realize was that I would remake that parachute many times over in crafting the Relational Finance model.

Relational Finance enables cost-effective access to finance capabilities without the inherent conflicts embedded in transactional models, and one of the many benefits of Relational Finance is being able to better utilize the traditional models with a partner on your side of the table with "other side" experience.

Through Relational Finance, every business that works with First Water becomes a partner company, irrespective of the nature of the relationship and associated economics. Partners are two (or more) people aligned around a shared goal, and who benefit if that goal is achieved. Whether a business owner wants to complete a project, explore and execute a transaction, or partners in the traditional sense of ownership, we always act with an ownership mentality in helping companies advance their story.

The best part of finance is storytelling, and telling your story through the lens of finance is the only way to attract the capital to achieve your growth and monetization objectives. When presented properly, business owners can address multiple capital audiences with confidence and pave a path to accomplishing their vision and monetizing their success.

At First Water, we leverage data and processes to promote and support the human components of finance, including a culture of accountability, goal setting, and storytelling. The purpose of data is dialogue, empowering teams with visibility, proactivity, and a way to plot the path.

When we identify what success looks like, the destination of our growth and capital roadmaps, we know that a confident decision is one that takes the next step along those paths. No matter how onerous or ambitious the journey, knowing that the next step is in the direction of the destination builds confidence and reduces stress. That is real value.

We have reached the end of this story, and I hope it serves as a catalyst to unleash your finance function. Relational Finance has proven to advance businesses through better teams, better growth, and better deals, and we are just getting started. Thank you for joining me on this journey to explore how Relational Finance is redefining finance for small and midsize businesses.

ABOUT FIRST WATER

REDEFINING FINANCE:
CONNECTING TEAMS WITH DATA AND COMPANIES WITH CAPITAL

First Water is a Relational Finance firm that partners with aspirational small and midsize businesses (SMBs) in their pursuit of growth, funding, transaction execution, and a better quality of life throughout the entrepreneurial journey. We are a one-stop shop for finance capabilities with the people and the toolbox to harness data, see around the corner, plot the course, confidently engage with capital, and boldly execute on transaction opportunities.

As the creator of Relational Finance, founder Ben Lehrer has built First Water to deliver on his mission of empowering SMBs with finance capabilities historically reserved for larger companies or limited to rigid engagement frameworks. Fueled by the team's diverse backgrounds and the Relational Finance model, First Water offers cost-effective, flexible, and aligned finance solutions to accelerate SMBs toward their goals.

Teams and companies with big goals trust us to support and advocate for them at critical inflection points. We earn that trust by holding fast to our belief that putting relationships before numbers yields better numbers. When our partner companies win, we win.
